STEPPING INTO YOUR GEULAH

Dear You,

You are not the same woman who sat at last year's *Seder*.
You've worked so hard to become who you are today.
And this year, you are not walking out of *Mitzrayim* alone.

Your bestie in print for *Pesach* is right here, walking beside you.
Pesach is not just a holiday. It is a milestone. A personal story.
A collective story. A Jewish story. A story of *geulah*.

This season calls for intention. And let's be honest, it also comes
with endless lists and life on speed mode. Cleaning. Cooking.
Organizing. Hosting. Planning.
Holding it all together.

So we teamed up with incredible contributors and created
a *Pesach* edition that feels like a breath of fresh air.
Something thoughtful. Something real. Something you
can sit with for a few quiet minutes and feel inspired, strengthened,
and understood.

No *chametz* here. Only content we would genuinely
want to read ourselves.
This edition opens spring with renewed *emunah* and
a sharper sense of direction.

You will find practical inspiration
for a meaningful *Yom Tov* and a refreshing *Chol HaMoed*.
You will meet women who are choosing courage, clarity, and faith
in real life, not in theory.

If something in these pages touches you, share the magazine.
Tell a friend. Bring it to your women's gathering.
Gift it. Reach out to an author
whose words resonated with you.

Build a real connection. A real friendship.
And if you feel inspired, send feedback.
A few sincere words can strengthen someone
more than you realize. Every contributor poured
her heart and intention into her piece.

May this *Pesach* bring you protected energy,
meaningful joy, renewed *emunah*, and the courage to step
fully out of your own *Mitzrayim* with light, dignity,
and sisterhood.

We are women from all walks of life, walking with you.

*Naomi Journo &
The Team*

This Nissan, Do Not Stay Small

BY: DEVORAH SISSO

IN LOVING MEMORY OF MY FATHER,
NISSIM BEN LYDIA ZT"L.
MAY HIS NESHAMA HAVE ALIYAH.

To be honest, It feels like we're all sensing the weight of *Pesach* before it even arrives… Every year as we get closer to "D day" we begin to feel the overwhelming feelings of way too much to take care of with not enough time… The clincher for me is always that added feeling of not being connected spiritually to this holy time, and maybe I'm missing the point by being so consumed by the list of things to do that perhaps I'm missing out on the actual point of everything I'm doing… I know something deeper is unfolding and I want to be a part of it!

We are entering a *tekufa*. A season. A spiritual shift, whether we are conscious of it or not.

Time is not something that moves over us. It is something we move through. That is why there are periods when every day feels exactly the same. Not because nothing is happening, but because we are not changing. When we stay the same, life feels repetitive, heavy, suffocating. But the moment we shift even one small thing, waking up earlier, praying, eating better, taking a walk, choosing differently, everything feels different. We feel more alive.

When people feel empty, it is often because there is nothing new inside. There is a gaping space we keep trying to fill with food, outings, distractions, or pleasure. And it never works. Nothing outside of us can fill that place. Only our actions, our choices, and our willingness to do something different can.

Nissan is the month of *geulah*. Redemption. *Pesach* is not a story we tell once a year. It is happening now. Every woman is meant to see herself as if she is leaving *Mitzrayim* today. And *Mitzrayim* is not a place. It is a state of being. It is fear. Habit. Addiction. Living on autopilot and calling it life.

For a long time, I thought freedom meant escape. Rest. Getting away. But freedom is much deeper than that. Freedom is control. Freedom is deciding instead of reacting. Freedom is not needing the world's approval to feel worthwhile.

Nissan is the month of geulah. Redemption. Pesach is not a story we tell once a year. It is happening now. Every woman is meant to see herself as if she is leaving Mitzrayim today. And Mitzrayim is not a place. It is a state of being. It is fear. Habit. Addiction. Living on autopilot and calling it life.

Everything begins in the mind. When the mind shifts, life follows. *Chametz* lives there first. Not in the kitchen, but in the thoughts. *Chametz* is not the enemy. It is a symbol. Anything I fully rely on that is not Hashem becomes *chametz*. Control. Money. Situations. Relationships. Habits. The places I lean on instead of trusting *Hashem*.

When I clean *chametz*, I try to think clearly. I am removing fear from my heart. Fear of failure. Fear of not being accepted. Fear of letting go of who I have always been. And when *chametz* burns, I imagine those fears burning out of my life. Not symbolically. Practically.

That is when *Pesach* cleaning changes. Every room becomes another layer of the soul opening. Every action done with awareness becomes purification.

We are made of two parts. A body and a soul. The body speaks the language of pleasure, distraction, numbing. The soul speaks the language of *kedusha*, meaning, and truth. The body is not bad, but it cannot lead. When it leads, life becomes a cycle of desire and disappointment. The soul is infinite. Trying to fill an infinite soul with finite pleasures creates constant hunger.

That emptiness is not a punishment.

It is there to help us reroute, to give more attention to what we truly need to be happy, not some poor version of it.

That is why people who seem to have everything often feel empty, while someone with very little can feel deeply alive. It says that in the days before *Moshiach* people will not be hungry for food or physical pleasures but rather for the truth and connection to it..

Emunah is not certainty. It is knowing that *Hashem* is behind the door, even when it is quiet. Like a baby who panics when her mother leaves the room, even though she is still right there. We panic when we think *Hashem* is gone, and then we rush to place our security in other things. *Emunah* is saying, I know You are here, even when I do not feel You. I will not abandon my truth.

A free woman is the captain of her ship. She decides what goes into her mouth and what comes out. She decides who she spends her time with, puts her trust in and how she lives her days.. That is power.

Pesach is the reset. When we burn *chametz*, we burn the belief that we cannot change. Nissan carries the energy of redemption, but we must participate. *Hashem* says, all I need is your will. Your thirst. Your desire to be free. And I will open the way.

Stop shrinking yourself with "this is my life." Clean your house and your heart together. Feed yourself real food. Soul food.

Pesach is not about leaving Egypt. It is about leaving what keeps you small.

Air out your home.
Air out your soul.

If you do, you will taste freedom.

Devorah Sisso is an internationally acclaimed *Torah* educator, Motivational Speaker & Life-coach. Creator of the Breakthrough series. Born in Israel and raised in the United States. Her energetic and soulful presentations have inspired literally thousands of people from across the Jewish spectrum & from all walks of life.

 devorah_sisso
 DevorahSisso

The Dream I Carried for Years:
My Aliyah Story

BY: RINA DEUTSCH

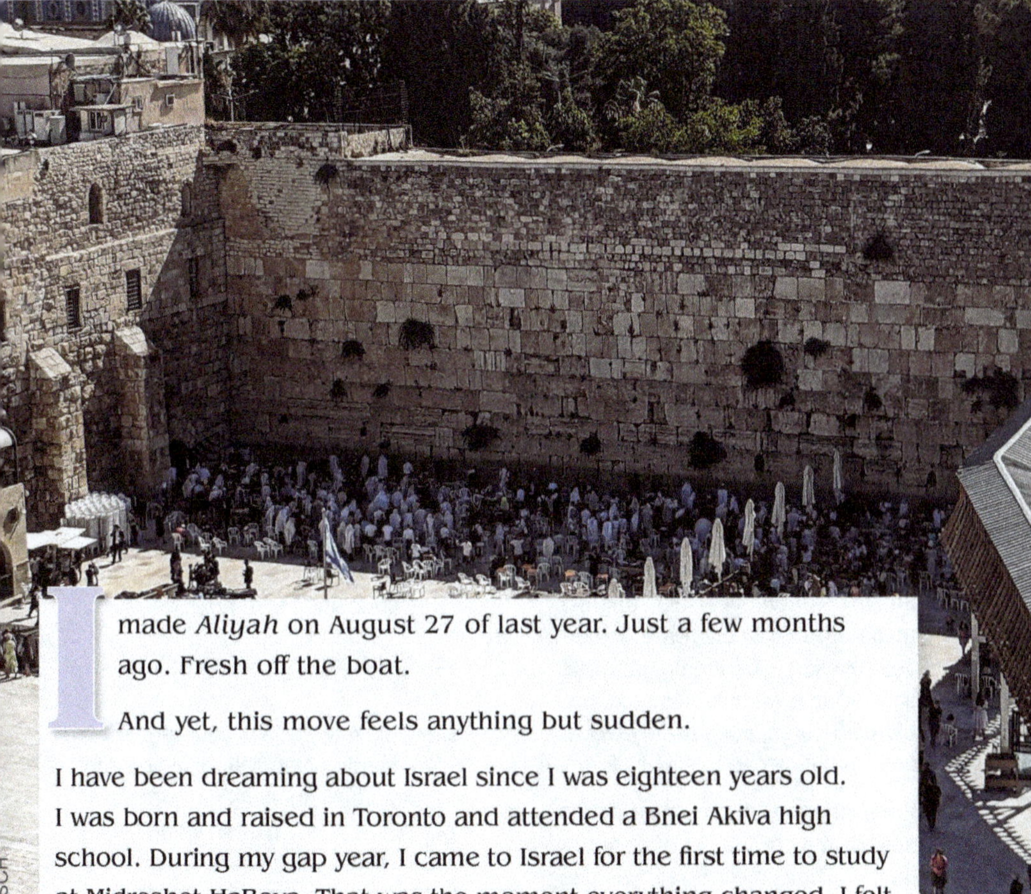

I made *Aliyah* on August 27 of last year. Just a few months ago. Fresh off the boat.

And yet, this move feels anything but sudden.

I have been dreaming about Israel since I was eighteen years old. I was born and raised in Toronto and attended a Bnei Akiva high school. During my gap year, I came to Israel for the first time to study at Midreshet HaRova. That was the moment everything changed. I felt it deep in my bones. This was where I was supposed to be.

Israel wasn't just a place I visited. It felt like home.

Over the years, there were several moments when I wanted to make *Aliyah*, but life never quite lined up. Timing, logistics, family responsibilities. Still, the dream never left me. I was the person watching *Nefesh B'Nefesh* videos on YouTube and crying, imagining a life I hadn't yet stepped into. I carried that longing quietly, through different seasons of life, always assuming that one day, somehow, it would finally happen.

THEN OCTOBER 7 HAPPENED. AND SOMETHING SHIFTED.

Spiritually, historically, emotionally, I felt an urgency I hadn't felt before. I wanted to be here with my people, for better or for worse. To be honest, I feel like I kind of know how the diaspora story for Jews ends. You can call me an alarmist if you want. But I didn't want to sit around and wait. This is my home, and I've known that since I was eighteen.

I'm divorced and a mother of five, and making *Aliyah* with children at very different stages of life was anything but simple. I came with "two and a half" of my kids. My twenty-year-old daughter and my fourteen-year-old daughter made *Aliyah* with me. My eighteen-year-old son is here on a gap year, still deciding what comes next. My two oldest children, ages twenty-two and twenty-four, chose to stay in Toronto.

What surprised me most was that it was actually my children who pushed me to do this. They've known for years that *Aliyah* was my dream. They watched me try, pause, and try again. One Friday night, we were sitting at the table when my oldest looked at me and asked,

"Why aren't you making *Aliyah*?" When I explained that my youngest wasn't sure, he replied, "She's thirteen. Since when does she make adult decisions?"

THAT MOMENT STAYED WITH ME.

They told me, "This is your moment. She's starting high school. If you don't go now, you'll be stuck for another four years." The children who wanted to stay said, "We'll figure it out." And we are figuring it out together, across time zones and life stages.

My fourteen-year-old wasn't thrilled at first, which is completely understandable.

Leaving friends, familiarity, and everything she knew was not easy. But she got on board. She's adapting beautifully, and I'm endlessly grateful for her courage and resilience.

We moved to Jerusalem, to the *Armon HaNatziv* neighborhood. Every morning, I walk my dog up a small hill near my home. If I turn left, I can see the Temple Mount. If I turn right, on a clear day, I can see the Dead Sea. It takes my breath away every single time. I know

that eighteen-year-old me would be so proud that I finally made this dream real.

I can even see that hill from my bedroom window. As *Pesach* approaches, the hills are already covered with purple lupines, one of the clearest signs that spring has arrived in Jerusalem.

The adjustment has been intense. The first few months were pure chaos. Everything felt urgent, unfamiliar, and emotionally charged. My mantra became *kacha zeh*. This is the way it is. Not in resignation, but in acceptance. With the right mindset, you can face uncertainty without letting it harden you.

My Hebrew is conversational, and I still have more to learn. My daughter's Hebrew was minimal when we arrived, so we found an English-language high school that integrates Hebrew learning in a supportive way. She's learning without drowning, and that has made all the difference for her confidence and sense of stability.

Professionally, *Aliyah* required reinvention. In Toronto, I spent seven years teaching Judaic studies at my high school alma mater. Here in Israel, thank G-d, I continue teaching at a seminary, alongside life-coaching work I've been doing internationally for several years. As a single mother supporting a family, necessity really is the mother of reinvention. I've worn many hats over the years, and I'm now also exploring new professional directions, including marketing, using skills I've developed through education, communication, and leadership.

Finding work here came down to one thing: networking. I reached out to people. I asked questions. I asked for introductions. I didn't wait to be discovered. Israel teaches you very quickly that initiative matters, and that doors often open through human connection. I even spoke to Hillel Fuld, a technology advisor, blogger, and vlogger, who really lives up to what he says. He jokes that if you make *Aliyah*, he'll get you a shawarma and help you find a job—and honestly, that's exactly the kind of attitude I encountered. People genuinely want to help.

One of the most surprising emotional rewards of *Aliyah* has been how little people care that I'm divorced. In Toronto, at least in my experience, there was more stigma.

Here, it's simply life. No judgment. No awkwardness. Just warmth, curiosity, and a genuine sense of belonging.

If I could offer advice to new *olim*, especially single mothers, it would be this: don't do *Aliyah* alone. Talk to people. Ask questions. Ask for help. Choosing the right community matters more than almost anything else. For single mothers in particular, my biggest advice is not to try to do everything yourself. Build a circle early, even if it feels uncomfortable. Israel is a place where help exists, but you have to be willing to ask for it.

As *Pesach* approaches, living in Israel feels especially meaningful. Not just as a story we tell, but as something we live. Leaving what's familiar. Stepping into uncertainty. Taking the leap before everything is clear. Trusting that freedom is worth the fear—because it is.

Rina Deutsch is a teacher, marketing strategist, and life coach supporting Jewish women and families through transition. A single mother of five, she recently made *aliyah*, blending faith, resilience, and humor as she builds a meaningful life and work in Israel.

 rinadeutsch@gmail.com
 @rinadeutsch

Beit Shemesh,
A Gentle Landing

BY DEVORAH BENARROCH

COURTESY OF DEVORAH BENARROCH
KIM BASH REAL ESTATE

INSET PHOTO BY TZIPORAH WAYNE

PHOTO BY HENNY LOKER

My journey to Beit Shemesh has been shaped by awakening, faith, and steady growth. In 2002, following the events of 9/11, I experienced a personal wake-up call that led me toward *teshuva* and ultimately to Israel. That moment reframed my sense of purpose, belonging, and the life I wanted to build, clarifying my desire for a life rooted in meaning, community, and Jewish continuity.

PHOTO BY RACHEL SCHREIBER LEVITAN

Women, Work, and Sisterhood

Women in Beit Shemesh are dynamic and resourceful. Many work remotely in education, therapy, marketing, tech, and coaching. Others run local businesses, teach, or balance part-time work with family life. Entrepreneurship is common, particularly among Anglo women, and collaboration often replaces competition.

Informal networking happens naturally through conversations, WhatsApp groups, women's gatherings, and community events. For many *olot*, this creates both professional opportunity and emotional grounding.

For mothers, flexibility is a major advantage. There is an unspoken understanding that family comes first. Women's circles, *shiurim*, workshops, and *chesed* initiatives are woven into everyday life. Whether helping a new *olah* navigate systems or quietly showing up when someone needs support, the *chesed* here feels sincere and human.

Education and Realities of Growth

Beit Shemesh offers a wide range of educational options, including *mamlachti dati*, *Torani*, *charedi*, Anglo-friendly frameworks, and special education programs. This diversity allows families to choose settings aligned with their values and their children's individual needs.

Although there are many English speakers, most schools function primarily in Hebrew. Preparing children linguistically makes a meaningful difference in confidence and integration.

Like many growing cities, some children find themselves between systems or questioning paths that differ from their parents' *hashkafa*. This is not unique to Beit Shemesh. The strength of the city is that support exists through professionals, community initiatives, and informal networks. Families are not left alone in these moments.

I made *aliyah* through Nefesh B'Nefesh and married in 2004, beginning the work on building a Jewish home. Our first years were spent in Telzstone, where we lived for twelve meaningful years. Those years were filled with raising children, deepening roots, and learning how faith becomes part of daily life. Telzstone gave us a strong foundation, but as our family grew, we were ready for a new stage.

In 2018, we moved to Ramat Beit Shemesh. From the beginning, the city felt like a meeting point between past and future, between Anglo and Israeli cultures, between striving and settling. It was not just a new location. It felt like the next stage of the journey. What surprised me most was how quickly it became personal. Neighbors noticed you. Women reached out. There was a quiet sense of arriving where you were meant to be.

A Community With a Living Neshama

Beit Shemesh has a unique *neshama*. A typical day feels active yet grounded. School drop-offs, work, errands, Torah learning, and community life move side by side. The rhythm of life is full but not overwhelming. The city is home to Anglos and Israelis, young families and retirees, religious, traditional, and many points in between.

There is a strong sense of shared responsibility. Women support one another in practical ways, from meals during transitions to sharing guidance, connections, and encouragement. Support often happens quietly. Spiritually, the city allows space for different expressions of growth, which is especially important for *olim* adjusting to a new culture.

Housing and Neighborhood Life

Ramat Beit Shemesh is often considered a gentle landing place for Anglos because of its infrastructure and community planning. Schools, *shuls*, clinics, parks, and transportation are integrated into daily life.

I live in Ramat Beit Shemesh Alef in an older walk-up building. Our five-bedroom apartment offers space, strong community ties, and a sense of stability that feels right for our family. Alef is known for its strong Anglo presence and neighborly feel. People know one another and life feels connected.

Gimmel has a newer feel and a growing mix of Israelis and Anglos. Daled continues to expand quickly and reflects a more Hebrew-speaking and Chassidic presence alongside Anglos. Neve Shamir offers newer buildings, open views, and a diverse population at many life stages.

Beyond the city itself, nearby *moshavim* such as Givat Eden and Neve Michael offer quieter options while remaining connected. Housing ranges from older walk-ups to newer buildings and family homes, allowing people to choose both a space and a community that fit their values.

What Makes Beit Shemesh Different

Beit Shemesh offers balance. It moves at a gentler pace than Jerusalem while remaining rich in *Torah*, community, and opportunity. It offers affordability relative to larger cities, access to nature, and room to grow.

There was a quiet moment when I realized Beit Shemesh was not just where I lived, but where I was growing. Through its people and rhythm, this community has shaped my life. I have found friends, learning partners, collaborators, and a deep sense of belonging. It is a city that allows women to evolve, families to settle with intention, and individuals to feel supported while becoming who they are meant to be.

My prayer for women considering *aliyah* or a move within Israel is that you find not just an address, but a place that holds you. A community that allows you to build, contribute, and feel truly at home.

Devorah Benarroch is an entrepreneur, community builder, and *emunah*-centered wellness advisor based in Beit Shemesh. Since 2020, she has partnered with Kim Bash to support Anglos relocating to Israel, while working with wellness professionals, coordinating retreats such as *Maim Haim*, distributing Mitz *Chai* juices, and developing AI-powered business workshops.

🌐 JewishHealingNetwork.com

🌐 kimbash.com

▶ info@jewishhealingnetwork.com

FINANCIAL CLARITY in Israel

Small Steps That Build Real Security

BY: RIFKA LEBOWITZ

Many women feel overwhelmed or disconnected from their finances, especially busy mothers. This is very common. Life is full, there is work, family, and constant responsibility, and finances often become the thing we push aside. Sometimes it even works for us not to deal with it, and we leave it to someone else, often a husband.

One of the first things worth checking is whether this feeling existed before making *aliyah*. Were finances overwhelming back then, or did this start after the move? *Aliyah* adds real challenges. There is a language barrier, a new system, and unfamiliar financial products. Even capable, confident women can feel unsure when everything works differently.

The very first step to regaining clarity and confidence is awareness. Sitting down and understanding where you are right now. What do you actually have? What is going on financially? This step is not about fixing everything or making decisions immediately. It is simply about knowing your starting point.

Understanding the Financial Foundations in Israel

The basic financial foundations are the same everywhere. We need to live within our means. Nobody can build stability without that. In Israel, this awareness is even more important because the system can feel more complex and the cost of living can be challenging.

Managing money wisely and building long term stability requires understanding Israeli financial products and cultural norms. How people handle money is influenced by culture. In some countries, saving for children's college is a major priority. In Israel, higher education costs much less, so that focus shifts. Instead, buying an apartment often becomes the main long term goal.

When people understand what they actually need to be working toward in Israel, it becomes much easier to plan and build stability.

Budgeting as Support, Not Restriction

Budgeting often sounds scary or restrictive, almost the opposite of financial freedom. But when you look at the bigger picture, budgeting is part of building wealth and reaching goals.

A budget does not need to mean tracking every receipt or checking every *shekel*, rather it can be a framework that guides your decisions. It needs to be realistic. It should include space for enjoyment. Space for something you love and something your partner loves. It also needs to include the real costs of life, holidays, maintenance, repairs, and unexpected expenses.

When something breaks, it should not feel like a crisis. It should feel like something you planned for. That is what creates peace of mind. When budgeting allows you to take a vacation, handle repairs, or buy what you need without stress, it becomes empowering rather than limiting.

A Key Tool for Long Term Security: Keren Hishtalmut

One of the most powerful financial tools in Israel is *Keren Hishtalmut*. It is a minimum six year savings plan available through employment or for the self employed.

It is unique because it allows money to grow tax free. Typically, part of the money comes from your salary and part comes from your employer. Over time, this can grow into a significant sum. After six years, the money can be withdrawn as a lump sum with no tax on the growth.

It is an incredible long term investment tool and something many people use to build financial security in Israel. It does not exist in the same way abroad, which is why many *olim* are unfamiliar with it. If a job offers *Keren Hishtalmut*, it is a benefit worth taking

seriously. (Americans, please ask your CPA about this as you might be taxed in the US on the growth)

Common Financial Mistakes After Aliyah

One of the biggest mistakes people make is ignoring the big picture. *Aliyah* is a huge upheaval, and many people focus only on getting through the present. Long term planning, pensions, and savings get pushed aside, sometimes for years.

Another common mistake is keeping all money in the country you came from. The *shekel* has strengthened over time, and people who kept their money in foreign currencies have often lost buying power in Israel.

There is also a common belief that everyone in Israel lives in overdraft. It is a misconception that they don't have other money. While overdraft exists, many people also have assets in the form of investments, *Keren Hishtalmut* pension funds, and property. Being in overdraft does not mean someone has no financial stability, and it should not be treated as an excuse to live beyond your means.

Fear, Aliyah, and Facing the Numbers

Financial uncertainty is one of the biggest fears holding people back from making *aliyah*, especially families. Retirees often know what their pension looks like. Young adults are flexible. Families in between carry real responsibility, and that fear is valid.

The most effective way to reduce fear is to face the numbers. Write them down. What does life actually cost? How long will savings last? Do your skills match the Israeli job market? If not, what can be done in advance?

Looking at job listings, improving skills, learning Hebrew, and understanding realistic salaries all reduce fear. When people translate their lifestyle needs into numbers, uncertainty becomes manageable. No one can promise a job, but clarity builds confidence.

Talking About Money as a Team

Money needs to be a shared conversation. Many couples avoid discussing financial goals until a moment arrives when questions suddenly surface. What are we saving for? What are we investing in? What does success look like for us?

A calm and constructive approach matters. Start with facts. Share how you feel. Say what you need. Suggest a specific time to talk. No blame. No accusations. Just two people working together.

Money is not about one of the couple winning or losing. It is about partnership and building a life together.

When Money Feels Tight

When finances feel tight, the instinct is often to cut back. Sometimes that is necessary. But another important question is how to improve your situation long term.

Israel is a place where people create opportunities. Side businesses are normal. Growth is encouraged. There is only so much you can cut, but there is far less limit to how much you can grow. Becoming better at what you do, earning more, or creating something new can be more empowering than constant restriction.

Financial stability is not about perfection. It is about awareness, intention, and working on improving things.

Rifka Lebowitz is the founder of Living Financially Smarter in Israel and a trusted advisor to 40,000 members. A Certified Financial Planner (CFP®) and author of *Smarter Israeli Banking*, she helps individuals align finances with values and live confidently within Israel's unique financial system through practical guidance and clear planning.

🌐 **rifkalebowitz.com**
f **Living Financially Smarter in Israel**
📷 **IG: livingfinanciallysmarter**
in **Rifka Lebowitz CFP®**

From Desert to Springs:

Exploring Israel on Chol HaMoed

BY: RAY ELISHA

Israel may be a tiny, teeny country, but it offers an extraordinary range of landscapes and experiences. From vibrant cities and peaceful beaches to desert expanses, green hills, and ancient sites, every region tells a different story. *Chol Ha'Moed* is a wonderful time to step out, travel, and reconnect with the land of *Eretz Yisrael*. Whether heading south to the Negev, north to the Golan, or exploring Jerusalem and its surroundings, each trip offers moments of discovery, meaning, and joy.

Desert

If your *Pesach* vacation takes you south, starting at Ein Gedi is a must. Once a refuge for King *David*, **Ein Gedi** offers waterfalls, lush greenery, wildlife, and breathtaking desert scenery. Hike along scenic trails, pause by cascading waterfalls, and enjoy a picnic surrounded by nature.

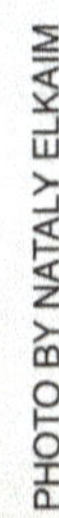

PHOTO BY NAOMI JOURNO

PHOTO BY NATALY ELKAIM

From there, drive south along the **Dead Sea** and marvel at the lowest point on Earth. **The Ein Bokek** area has several spots where you can stop, lather up in mineral-rich Dead Sea mud, and soak in the naturally warm waters.

With that blissful, post-spa feeling, continue south to **Mitzpe Ramon's Alpaca Farm**. Born out of a dream to raise gentle, unique animals for companionship, Ilan and Naama Dvir founded the farm in the 1970's. Visitors can feed, interact with and learn about alpacas and llamas while observing them in a calm, natural environment.

The perfect way to end the trip is at the **Ramon Crater** lookout. Just a short drive away, the crater opens up to vast desert views by day and spectacular stargazing after sunset. Join a guided stargazing tour or simply pull over, look up, and let the desert sky work its quiet magic.

☑ TRIP TIPS

What makes the **Ramon Crater** unique is that it was formed by erosion from an ancient ocean, rather than by volcanic or meteor activity. Take time to experience the immense scale of this rare geological phenomenon.

A beautiful sunset viewing point is **Camel Hill** lookout, which faces south over a bend in the crater. As day turns to night, it offers a breathtaking transition worth lingering for.

Jerusalem

Tucked just ten minutes from the outskirts of Jerusalem, in the Judean Hills, lies **Sataf**, a historical site known for its natural beauty and ancient agricultural practices. Ideal for outdoor enthusiasts, **Sataf** features hiking trails, bicycle paths, picnic areas, two natural springs, and even a French-style bakery and patisserie.

The site also includes the *Eretz Yisrael Tree Garden*, where cultivated fruit trees grow in their original, indigenous varieties. At **Ein Sataf**, one of the natural springs, visitors can enter a cave from which the spring flows and walk through a tunnel that opens on the other side. Be sure to bring a flashlight or candles.

Afterwards, follow the green trail to the second spring, **Ein Bichora**, and climb through the ancient ruins of the **Sataf** village toward the trailhead. Along the way, you'll notice an ancient wine press and agricultural terraces still irrigated, using traditional methods. For thousands of years, these terraces allowed water to flow naturally between plots, sustaining crops on the hillside.

Return during the summer to see the springs running alongside vine, fig, and olive trees that dot the Jerusalem hills.

☑ TRIP TIPS

Sataf has three free parking lots. **Ein Karem** is only a five to ten-minute drive away and makes for a lovely stop before or after your visit. During *chag*, you may find performances, events, or open cafés worth exploring.

North

If you're looking for sweeping views, rich greenery, and a chance to rest and reset during *chag*, northern Israel offers all of this and more.

In the Upper Golan Heights lies the **Banias Nature Reserve**, a site that goes far beyond the typical park experience. A powerful spring emerges from the base of Mount Hermon and flows for approximately 3.5 kilometers through a gorge, eventually forming a dramatic waterfall.

The reserve includes two main areas: the springs and the waterfall. Four hiking trails range from 45 to 90 minutes, allowing visitors to choose their level of adventure. The Banias waterfall is Israel's largest, plunging ten meters downward. Stand on the observation deck, close your eyes, and feel the cool mist rise as the water crashes below.

Along the trails, you'll encounter fascinating points of interest, including a hot spring, an operational flour mill with olive press facilities, and moats dating back to the Crusader and Mameluke periods.

☑ TRIP TIPS

Chol Ha'Moed weather is usually ideal, with temperatures ranging from 18-25°C (64-77°F).

The reserve is home to diverse wildlife, including birds and snakes. Observe from a safe distance.

Admission, parking, and on-site food require payment.

☑ EXTRA TIPS

A few special experiences take place specifically during *Chol Ha'Moed*. One highlight is the **Moshav Festival**, also known as the **Moshav County Fair**. Located between Jerusalem and Tel Aviv, this year marks the festival's 20th anniversary, celebrating unity, spirit, hope, and beauty among the Jewish people.

Another meaningful stop is **Emunah Matzah Bakery in Netivot**. Located in the Gaza Envelope, this unique bakery weaves *Pesach* tradition together with the strength, resilience, and faith of its surrounding community, offering visitors both insight and inspiration.

Ray Elisha is a writer whose dream is to own a communal bookstore and to live on a large plot of land. She envisions rehabilitating animals, offering vegan education and cooking classes; and raising a tribe of loving, adventurous children—all guided by her deep connection to Israel and Judaism

MATZAH MINDSET:
A PESACH INVITATION TO RESET OUR RELATIONSHIP WITH FOOD

BY: CHANA GORENSTEIN

Every time *Pesach* rolls around, I get that feeling.

Not the familiar stress of cleaning, the pressure to come up with new recipes, or the endless shopping lists. That too, of course. Which Jewish mom does not deal with that?

Alongside it, another feeling arises, one of awe, gratitude, and quiet excitement all at once. I am not sure it even has a name.

That feeling does not come from the to-do list. It comes from an experience I had almost nine years ago that aligns deeply with the spiritual timing of this holiday and with the season we find ourselves in: spring.

For many years, I was stuck in my relationship with food. Unaware of the depth of my own internal *golus*, I was caught in a web of unhealthy habits and addictive patterns, eating impulsively and haphazardly, to say the least. Whatever I wanted. Whenever I wanted. Wherever I wanted.

That lack of self-awareness lasted a long time before catching up with me. Years. Decades, really. It felt endless, certainly longer than 210 years, until I experienced my own inner *Yetziat Mitzrayim*, an exodus from low-level food behaviors that quietly set the stage for real personal growth.

For many people, their relationship with food genuinely feels like a battle. The *Zohar* refers to eating as a *milchama*, a battlefield of inner struggle, so much so that it says we should engage it with the edge of a sword.

The word *meitzar*, the root of *Mitzrayim*, means constriction. When we are caught in harmful cycles or negative habits, we experience that same sense of confinement, the disorientation of exile. We feel imprisoned by our behaviors.

But just as *Hashem* promised the *Yidden* that they would not remain imprisoned and took every Jew out, the same is true of our personal exiles. We can leave our own food *golus* behind, especially at this time of year.

Thank G-d, *Pesach* is here. Our sages teach that when a holiday returns, it brings with it the spiritual energy of the original experience. *Pesach* is a time of renewal. Of liberation. Of fresh starts. It carries the power to jump out of patterns that once felt impossible to escape.

How do we begin to break free from habits that have kept us stuck for years, sometimes decades?

Change begins with awareness. As long as our eating happens automatically, the cycle stays intact. *Pesach* interrupts our food habits in a simple but powerful way. We can't just grab what we want. We can't eat whatever we want, whenever we want, without thinking. There are boundaries around what we are allowed to eat and when. This creates an opportunity to pause, to step back, and to see what is working and what isn't in our eating habits.

In addition, we are forced to simplify our eating, just as *matzah* is prevented from rising. *Matzah* represents simple, unlayered eating patterns. *Chametz*, on the other hand, rises and puffs itself up, much like the layers of self-protection our eating patterns are often built on. When those layers are stripped away through self-awareness, internal growth becomes possible.

One simple way to interrupt the cycle is to write things down. Try keeping a food journal for one week. Write what you eat, when you eat, and what was going on for you at the time. Don't change anything yet. Just notice. Patterns become clear very quickly

when they're on paper, and awareness is what opens the door to real change.

It is no coincidence that *Pesach* occurs in the spring, when the world begins to bloom. Growth unfolds gradually, and the same is true for personal change.

One of the fundamental truths of growth is that it takes time. We often expect change to happen instantly, even though the Jews left Egypt in a single moment and still needed fifty days to reach the purpose of the Exodus. A flower does not bloom overnight. Neither do we. When we remember that, it becomes much easier to stay the course.

Another truth of growth is that it includes difficulty. Before a seed becomes a flower, it breaks open. Beginnings are hard. Growth spurts hurt. Yet we often expect ourselves to push through without acknowledging that pain. Growth is easier when we water the process with compassion, especially when the going gets hard.

This is especially true when we face cravings. In those moments, we want to stay aligned with our higher goals, yet we often fold. If we remember that difficulty is part of growth—even calling it to mind through visualization, imagining ourselves as a seed breaking down— and respond with gentleness rather than force ("I am having a growth spurt now. This hurts, but I am going to be okay"), the moment softens, the urge passes, and we can continue forward.

And there is one more essential ingredient without which nothing can grow.

Without *Hashem* infusing the earth with the power to grow, the seed remains a seed. Without *Hashem* taking us out of Egypt, the Yidden would have remained stuck.

Internally, this means aligning with our *neshama*, the G-dly spark within us that carries infinite potential. When growth is approached from that place, change is not only possible—it is lasting.

Acceptance, compassion, and trust create the soil in which real change can take root.

So the next time you face a craving or an obstacle, remember to A.C.T. Accept that growth takes time. Water the process with compassion. Trust the One who makes growth possible.

And then, slowly and quietly, we can re-experience that feeling.
The feeling of freedom.

Chana Gorenstein is a Chabad *shlucha*, *Torah*-based food and habit coach, educator, writer, and founder of **SoulCare**. She helps Jewish women end the war inside and build stable, boundaried relationships with food—*Yiddishkeit* applied all the way down to the plate—where food habits, emotional regulation, and *Torah* values intersect in real life.

🌐 **soul-care.co.il**
▶ **chanagorenstein@gmail.com**
🟢 **WhatsApp group:**
    SoulCare-TLC Training
    Private message to join

A Cup of Spring

Blooming teas, fresh flavors, and easy spring blends

BY TOVIT KELLY

Chag HaAviv

Working with herbs in the rhythms of nature became an integral part of my life long before I understood the physical properties of botanicals. Seeing a "weed" like dandelion or purslane and realizing it carries a lineage of healing stretching back centuries awakened something deep within me.

I instinctively felt safe in nature and drawn to the plants and trees. Over time, I explored, studied, and applied nature's lens to the emotional and spiritual realms, discovering deeper connection and support for the physical body.

Spring, Pesach, and Herbal Tradition

Spring is a powerful season of renewal, hope, rebirth, optimism, and new beginnings. These themes are deeply connected to *Yetziat Mitzrayim*, the Exodus. *Pesach* arrives during this season and celebrates the spiritual counterpart of nature's awakening.

Pesach and herbalism intertwine through the ritual use of bitter herbs, *maror*, such as romaine and horseradish, symbolizing the bitterness of slavery, alongside green herbs like parsley and *karpas*, representing spring, growth, and life.

These practices are rooted in Biblical tradition and remind us that freedom is both physical and spiritual.

The days grow longer, the sun shines brighter, and nature awakens from its winter stillness, inspiring renewed vitality.

Spring is traditionally a time to support movement and flow within the body. After the slower winter months, systems such as circulation, the liver, kidneys, and lymphatic flow may feel more stagnant. Herbal teas offer a gentle and nourishing way to align with the season and support the body as it transitions.

All ingredients in the tea blends listed are sourced as pure, whole, single dried herbs, blossoms, leaves, berries, roots, and/or spices, and are unflavored. Some herbs are considered medicinal.

Please note: If additional ingredients such as flavors are added, they should be reliably certified kosher and kosher for Pesach.

Key Seasonal Herbs for Simple Infusions:

Nettle, dandelion, red clover, rose petal or bud, lavender bud, hawthorn, violet, plantain, elderflower, lemon balm, peppermint, hibiscus, cinnamon, chamomile, citrus.

Spring Herbal Tea Preparations:

Tea Blending

These blends are designed to support overall wellness and are suitable for all ages and stages.
Fun, nourishing, and worth trying.

Spring Awakening

Ingredients:

Dried hibiscus, dried rose petals, dried elderflower, orange slices

Tasting notes: Tart, floral, and bright

Benefits: Rich in antioxidants and supportive of immune health (*hibiscus is known to reduce blood pressure. Avoid if on medication for hypertension or diabetes)

Gentle Detox

Ingredients:
2 parts dandelion root, 2 parts nettle, 1 part mint, 1 part rose

Tasting notes: Earthy, fresh, and lightly floral

Benefits: Supports gentle movement and flow in the body and provides mineral nourishment

Desert Oasis Digestive Blend

Ingredients:
Dandelion root, cinnamon chips or broken stick, ginger root, fennel seed, rose petal

Tasting notes: Warm, spicy, and naturally sweet

Benefits: Traditionally used to ease digestion, reduce bloating, and support gut comfort

How to Make Your Blends:

Combine: Mix the herbs of your chosen blend in a bowl. Store any remaining dried blend in a sealed jar in a cool, dark place.

Steep: Use 1 to 2 teaspoons of the blend per cup, 8 oz, of hot water.

Infuse: Pour boiling water over the herbs, cover, and steep for 5 to 15 minutes.

Strain and serve: Enjoy plain, or add honey or lemon to taste.

Wishing you a joyful spring and *Chag Sameach*

> **Disclaimer**
> *This information is for educational purposes only.*
>
> *These products are not intended to diagnose, treat, cure, or prevent any disease.*
>
> *Always consult a qualified healthcare professional before adding herbal supplements to your routine, especially if you are pregnant, nursing, taking prescription medications, or have a pre-existing medical condition.*

Tovit Kelly is the founder and herbalist of **Earth's Abundant Apothecary**. She is passionate about the plant world, foraging, and crafting small batch botanical products, from elixirs and electuaries to oxymels, infusions, body oils, and bath brews. She hosts herbal workshops and guides others along their plant path.

🌐 **earthsabundance.square.site**
📷 **earthsabundance.apothecary**
▶ **earthsabundance.apothecary@ gmail.com**

3 SOMATIC SHIFTS TOWARD GEULAH

BY: MIRIAM RACQUEL FELDMAN

Many years ago, as I sat sleepily at the *seder* table *Pesach* night, I came across some beautiful insight from the Lubavitcher Rebbe in Rabbi Miller's *Toras Menachem Haggadah*: "Judaism is, essentially, a 'feminine' religion. As a religious and ethical system, it seeks to change the world into a better place, but its approach to achieving this goal is a uniquely feminine one." (based on *Likutei Sichos*, vol 20, p.218).

29

I had already begun my coach/somatic training, and these words fit precisely into the journey I was on. Previously, I had been suffering from aches and pains all over my body and ran from doctor to chiropractor to massage therapist to seek relief. But to no avail. Time spent, money exchanged, and relief was short lived.

One day, the massage therapist placed her hand on my collarbone and said, "There is nothing here. You are empty." It was an "aha" moment for me. I realized that this physical pain was a symptom of a much deeper problem. My life force had been drained.

In my dazed state at the *Pesach* table, I asked myself what was the *Mitzrayim* that I was in and needed to leave? Over the years, had I been growing as a Jewish woman in the way of the feminine—nurturing and gentleness, or in the way of the masculine— conquering and subduing? The answer was obvious—I had been treating myself harshly by overworking, by people-pleasing, and by degrading myself with unkind, critical language.

In the years that have passed, I have rebirthed myself many times over. Every day, I make the effort to step out of *Mitzrayim* and release the shackles of *Golus* and step onto a more *Geulah* path of healing.

Hashem doesn't stop sending growth opportunities to refine me or any of us as souls in bodies, but there are doable shifts that we can make to create a more compassionate journey for ourselves. A more feminine, nurturing energy to bring into the world.

Incorporating the wisdom of the body is the somatic/mindbody approach that helps us on this *Geulah* journey.

Let's take a look at 3 shifts to help us step out of our own *Mitzrayim* and embrace the awesome healing powers we have within:

MITZRAYIM 1:
OVERWORKING AND IGNORING THE BODY

Our thoughts are not always true and can act like quite the slave drivers. They can push us harder than our bodies can endure and affect the body's actual physical state.

We can choose to do everyday tasks with a sharp focus—like a lioness on the hunt, ears forward, eyes sharply focused, adrenaline and cortisol racing through her system—or a soft focus—more breath, more space, less intensity. We can choose a different energy by adjusting our thoughts and being kind to our bodies.

Combining the Rebbe's teaching that Judaism is a feminine religion based on nurturing and gentleness with an understanding of the human nervous system, you can bring out your best self in making changes.

Try this: Replace "have to" with "choose to"

If you have a to-do list a mile long and a "have-to" list twice as long, then you are not bringing awareness of the positive limitations of your body. You are being a slave driver to the gift that *Hashem* has bestowed upon you—your body.

Toggle between the two phrases and feel the effects on your body:

"I have to get this and this done."

or

"I choose to get this and this done."

Notice that with "have to" there can be a sense of fear, dread, alarm, pressure, and/or tension—like a sharp focus.

With "choose to," there may be more expansion in your chest and more space in your mind—a softening of sorts. Put your hands on your chest, release a long breath out, and pause before breathing back into your stomach. Rewrite your list with the word "choose."

You may be thinking, "choose to" sounds nice, but there are things that "have to get done!" Yes, things have to get done, but technically, everything is a choice. We choose to do things because we want a certain positive outcome or are avoiding a negative outcome. We can "choose to" do laundry because we'd like clean clothes to wear, and we can "choose to" pay bills to avoid late fees. Healthy language and words are important for the body and soul.

MITZRAYIM 2: PEOPLE-PLEASING

When we people-please, we are making someone else our god. This is a type of *avodah zorah* and probably one of

the worst kinds because we tend to ignore the wisdom of our bodies and intuition and only react from fear of what someone else may think of us.

Contemplate this: "My value as a person is independent of what any mortal thinks of me."—Rabbi Pliskin

Hashem sees everything—who we are and what is going on in our lives—He is the one we account to.

I once had a friend with Borderline/Grandiose tendencies who continually asked for favors. I was too uncomfortable to say, "no," though I was overwhelmed with things in my life. I didn't want to appear ungenerous, selfish, or lose her friendship. I was more fearful of her than of *Hashem*, who knew my energy level and the other things that I was dealing with in my life.

Saying "no" and using our G-d-given *gevurah* (pulling back, discipline) allows for *chesed* (an expansion, kindness) to ourselves, to our families, and to projects that are part of our soul missions. We can leave our people-pleasing tendencies back in *Mitzrayim* where they belong and choose *yiras shomayim* and health instead.

MITZRAYIM 3: DEGRADING SELF WITH UNKIND, CRITICAL LANGUAGE

Celebrate yourself—instead of beating yourself up—for your efforts throughout your day. Put your hands above your head in a "V" shape (for victory!) and say, "Yay me! Thank you, *Hashem*!" This is a somatic technique which brings endorphins, the feel-good hormones,

to the brain with more blood flow and oxygen.

I give this "Yay, me! Thank you, *Hashem*" exercise to my clients with the invitation to do it often. The prescription is at least 3 times a day! Doing this creates new neural pathways in your mind. You are nurturing your divine essence and helping bring out your best self.

When you prepare for *Pesach* this year, may it be with kindness to yourself. May you leave behind your internal shackles of *Golus* and step into *Geulah* with renewed strength at your *Pesach* table.

Miriam Racquel Feldman transforms women's lives through somatic healing as an award-winning author, dating and marriage coach, and trauma and anxiety specialist. Her innovative, body-based approach has helped thousands heal relationships, resolve trauma, gain career clarity, and reconnect with inner wisdom and joy.

Books: God Said What?! #MyOrthodoxLife; Somatic Healing for the Modest Goddess.

MiriamRacquel.com

YourMarriageMagic.com

LEAVING EGYPT IS A PRACTICE

BY: LEIGH LOFFE

> " IN EVERY GENERATION, WE ARE MEANT TO SEE OURSELVES AS IF WE PERSONALLY LEFT EGYPT. "

For most of my life, that line felt abstract. I didn't understand why I was meant to see myself through the lens of a slave who was freed. What did that story have to do with my life?

We know that the word Egypt (*Mitzrayim*) comes from the root *meitzar*, meaning narrow or constricted places. Leading up to the Exodus, the Jewish people were enslaved, held down, and constricted not only physically, but emotionally and spiritually. Egypt wasn't only a place. It was a state of being.

Ah. Now this, I could understand.

Many women know these states of constriction all too well: chronic overwhelm, overfunctioning, people-pleasing… anxiety, depression, addiction, and for some, thoughts of suicide. We look functional. We show up. We perform our roles. But inside, we feel narrowed and cut off from our full selves and from a sense of wholeness. When these states persist, life can begin to feel like an exile.

My relationship with these inner exiles has been both personal and professional. I can't remember a time in my life when anxiety wasn't present. From a young age, it shaped how I moved through the world. I learned how to function with it by overworking, overfunctioning, and numbing. I believed that if I stayed productive and useful, the discomfort would eventually loosen its grip. (Spoiler alert: it didn't.)

At twenty-three, facing the end of a painful and unhealthy marriage, that strategy collapsed. I could no longer outrun what was happening inside me. For the first time, I had to look honestly at the inner constriction I had been living in for years.

At the same time, I was immersed in my professional role as a director for CTeen, a global Jewish youth organization. I worked closely with teens, parents, rabbis, and rebbetzins, and I witnessed how many young people were struggling—often silently—with anxiety, depression, self-harm, and suicidal thoughts. These weren't abstract conversations. These were real people I knew and cared about.

That intersection—between my own inner *Mitzrayim* and the suffering I was witnessing in my community—became my entry point into suicide prevention education.

I made a conscious decision to take responsibility for what I could change. I sought out training in suicide prevention and crisis response so I could better support the people I loved. I learned how to ask hard questions directly and compassionately, how to recognize warning signs, and how to sit with someone in pain without minimizing it. At the same time, I began my own healing journey, immersing myself in education on interpersonal neurobiology, attachment, trauma, and expressive and creative practices to help release me from my inner straits.

Over time, this work became the foundation for The Long Short Road, the nonprofit I founded in 2019, dedicated to suicide prevention and mental wellness education. Every day, we walk alongside women on their healing journeys, helping them step out of narrow places and into greater expansion and wholeness.

What I've learned—through both lived experience and professional training—is that when emotional pain overwhelms the nervous system, the system contracts. Thinking becomes rigid. Options disappear. *Meitzar.* In deep emotional pain, it becomes difficult to see a way out. Suicidal thoughts are rarely about wanting to die. They are about wanting the pain to stop. They are signals that the system no longer feels safe.

Healing doesn't begin with advice or solutions. It begins with connection. It begins with feeling, in the words of Dr. Daniel Siegel, "seen, safe, soothed, and secure."

The Exodus story reflects this. Redemption didn't begin with the miracles of the Ten Plagues. It began with a sigh—with the Israelites finally exhaling their pain and allowing it to be heard:

"And the children of Israel sighed from the labor, and they cried out… G-d heard their cry… and G-d knew." (*Shemot* 2:23–25)

The entry point into redemption from our exiles is acknowledging our pain with compassion and allowing ourselves to be seen with compassion. Hashem saw their pain, and that was the very beginning of freedom.

When a woman feels emotionally safe, her nervous system can settle. Her breath deepens. Her thinking softens. Possibility begins to return. Expansion happens through safety and connection, not pressure or urgency.

HOW TO SUPPORT A WOMAN WHO IS STRUGGLING

Everyone can play a role in preventing suicide.

Listen for invitations. Notice changes in tone, withdrawal, or self-critical language. These are often bids for connection.

Speak with compassion and clarity. If you're worried, say so. Asking directly about suicidal thoughts can create relief rather than fear.

Offer presence, not solutions. Resist the urge to fix. Sit with her. Listen without judgment. Avoid moralizing or shaming her pain.

Widen the circle of support. Help her identify others who can support her. Do not carry this alone.

If you or someone you care about is struggling with thoughts of self-harm or suicide, please reach out for support. Talk to someone you trust or seek professional help. You are not alone. We are here for you.

I know this to be true from my own life and from the hundreds of women I have walked alongside over the years. Change rarely comes from a "huge" shift. More often, it comes from the quiet stillness of being met exactly as we are.

So what are small ways you can begin, right here and right now, to add softness and expansiveness to your narrow places? Start with a breath. Connect with your body. Speak to yourself with compassion. Hug yourself. Find ways to add joy and expansiveness into your day, in small ways. Personally, I like expressive writing, listening to a *shiur*, or building Lego. For you, it might be a moment of quiet reflection in nature. Don't wait for a big breakthrough. Start here. Start now. Start with an exhale.

Leigh Loffe is a wife, mom to three delicious girls, a taco enthusiast, and an avid Lego builder. She is the founder and director of The Long Short Road, where she supports women through suicide prevention education, psychoeducation, and relational mental health support.

🌐 **thelongshortroad.org**
📞 **Warmline: 484-474-0544**
  Sun-Thurs 10am-10pm,
  Winter Fri 10am-3pm;
  Summer Fri 10am-6pm (all EST)

REAL COFFEE TALK: CANCER, UNFILTERED

WITH

Shari MENDES

Rachel SILVERMAN

HER TRIBE MAGAZINE

FOR REFUAH SHLEIMA OF MICHAELA LEEBA BAT HENDEL BLIMA

Life doesn't always follow the plans we make, and sometimes we face challenges we never wished for. In sharing this conversation, we hope to offer support and perspective. Shari Mendes, an architect by profession and founder of The Lemonade Fund, Israel's first and only breast cancer emergency relief fund, is also an IDF reservist who has been on duty since October 7, supporting families through moments of profound loss.

Alongside her is Rachel Silverman, a Sharsheret Midwest Chapter Advisory Committee Member, devoted mother of four, and a Chicago native preparing to make *Aliyah* to Israel.

Having both walked through cancer and healed, they chose to turn their experiences into helping others. Whether you are seeking guidance or simply wish to listen and understand, we invite you to join this conversation. May we all be blessed with health.

WHEN YOU FIRST HEARD THE DIAGNOSIS, HOW DID YOU HANDLE THE INITIAL FEAR, AND WHAT HELPED YOU TAKE THE VERY FIRST STEP FORWARD?

SHARI: My breast cancer was diagnosed during a routine mammogram at age 49. I have no family history and was not particularly concerned, so this news came as a tremendous shock. I was terrified, but a few things helped contain the fear. I first turned to my faith in G-d, reassuring myself that fear and faith could coexist; that fear was normal in such a life-threatening situation, and that even those who had been given reassurance directly from G-d, such as Yaakov and Joshua, were still afraid when facing danger. I prayed that I would survive the disease in order to see my children grow up. I remember praying to see grandchildren.

Secondly, I was fortunate to have a good support system. My husband is a surgeon, and he was then and has been my steady rock throughout. My medical team was very good; they cared about me and I trusted them. I chose to keep my health situation private for a year, but my family and close friends were very supportive of me.

Despite all of this, it was very difficult for me, very scary. I think this challenge changed me, giving me a new understanding of how people keep moving forward in the face of tremendous challenges.

RACHEL: I went for my first-ever mammogram on my 40th birthday. At that visit, they told me not to be alarmed if I was called back, as they did not have prior scans to compare to. Several follow-up visits later, I was shocked to be confronting the reality that no woman wants to hear, especially as a young mother with no family history: I had breast cancer.

My worst fear was needing to verbally express to my husband and my kids the words, "I have cancer." I was afraid that my husband and kids would think I was going to die. I was afraid that they would see me as sick and that I couldn't be the wife and mother to them that I always had been and always wanted to be.

Once I confronted my fears and told my family, we connected with an incredible Jewish medical community in Chicago, including Sharsheret, and began meeting with doctors to map out a treatment plan. Turning fear into action gave me a sense of control, and from that point on, I was determined to stay strong, positive, and grateful as I faced this unexpected challenge.

IN THE EARLY STAGES, HOW DID YOU CHOOSE YOUR MEDICAL TEAM, AND WHAT ADVICE WOULD YOU GIVE WOMEN WHO FEEL OVERWHELMED BY MEDICAL DECISIONS?

RACHEL: Based on the experiences of other women in my community who had recently battled breast cancer, I was immediately connected with one medical team (surgeon, oncologist, plastics) that was part of the main local hospital network. After meeting with them, I felt that I wanted to get a second opinion regarding treatment options, so I reached out to the incredible resources in our community for suggestions and connections.

I was advised to reach out to a group of women doctors, all in their young 40s, who had recently helped several women in our community. I met with them and immediately knew this was the medical team I wanted in charge of my care. I could relate to them on a real, personal level, and it made me feel like these doctors were human beings, not just disconnected medical professionals working on another patient. From that first meeting and for the next year-plus, these women were my guardian angels.

Once I made the decision as to my medical team, I never felt overwhelmed because I took things one day at a time, never feeling like I couldn't ask a question and only focusing on the immediate challenge in front of me.

SHARI: I was fortunate that my husband worked in a hospital, so we already had a network of trusted specialists in the surgery department. I learned early that Google and breast cancer online sites only panicked me, so I would recommend staying away from such general information that doesn't fit everyone. I spoke to other friends who had been through similar experiences, and at times this was helpful.

I spent a bit of time researching oncologists at different health centers. I interviewed a few of them after getting recommendations. Once I decided to move forward with an oncologist, I made peace with trusting them. I recommend not scrimping on this step and even paying privately for that one-time consultation if needed. It is money well spent; it is important to have faith in the doctor who will be shepherding one's oncological treatment.

HOW DID YOU BALANCE TRUSTING YOUR DOCTORS WHILE ALSO LISTENING TO YOUR OWN BODY AND INTUITION THROUGHOUT TREATMENT?

SHARI: I read one book, Anti-Cancer by Dr. David Servan-Schreiber, and followed his instructions about healthy eating and staying healthy in general. His advice helped me get through treatment and helps me to this day. I recommend this book to everyone, cancer patients and not.

It is not simple to listen to one's body during that initial period, as there is a feeling that the body betrayed you (at least that is how I felt). I also felt that perhaps I hadn't been listening well enough since I was so shocked by the diagnosis. In time, I learned to accept and not blame myself. Nothing I knowingly did caused my cancer, and it was important to be gentle and kind to myself, whether that meant exercising or resting. Swimming and walking helped a great deal, as did allowing myself to watch some good TV series.

RACHEL: I was fortunate to have a medical team that treated me in a way where I did not feel like I was ever being dictated to. They validated my questions and feelings while providing me with their expert medical recommendations. It is very important to share with your loved ones and your medical team how you are feeling and what you are thinking at all times so that everyone is on the same page for each step of the journey.

DURING TREATMENT, WHAT WERE SOME OF THE HARDEST DAYS, AND WHAT PRACTICAL TOOLS, HABITS, OR MINDSET SHIFTS HELPED YOU GET THROUGH THEM?

SHARI: Prayer, mindfulness, and as steady a routine as possible. I continued to work throughout my treatment (my work is not strenuous, and I am fortunate to work from home). This helped me a great deal.

RACHEL: For me, chemo was the hardest. The exhaustion, feeling sick, and not being able to be there for my kids, needing to stay in bed all day; it was all very hard. I knew the "hard days" were only a few out of each cycle, so I mentally prepared myself to handle the difficulties, knowing that I'd have better days ahead. The love and support of my family throughout helped me greatly as well.

Throughout my battle, from the early days of my diagnosis, I began to be more focused on my tefillah. I focused on davening not for a cure, but for the strength to get through things. I also got a great deal of strength from davening for other women going through breast cancer or similar health challenges.

How did you approach telling your children or close family about your illness, and what helped you navigate those conversations as a family?

SHARI: Telling my parents was very hard. I was so scared to hurt them, but they were wonderful and tremendously supportive. They were very strong and

helpful. I allowed my children to lead the discussion, answering questions as they asked them and not telling them more than they wanted to know. I reassured them that I was under very good care and doing everything possible. In the end, I think that if children see the family routine being as close to normal as possible (and I know that I was fortunate that this was possible for me), that is the most important thing to them.

RACHEL: As I mentioned earlier, my biggest fear was telling my family, especially my kids. The first thing I did was call my girls' therapist to ask how best to approach this conversation with my kids. I did not want to hurt them or scare them. Their therapist wisely told me that the most important thing was to be fully honest and transparent at all times, but to speak to each of my children at an age-appropriate level.

My kids, understandably scared and worried for their mother, were incredibly strong, supportive, and resilient throughout. I think the fact that I had open and honest communication with them, keeping them up to date throughout, each at their own level, helped them handle the burden and stress of having a mother battling breast cancer.

WHAT ROLE DID EMUNAH, OR INNER MINDSET, PLAY DURING THE MOST CHALLENGING MOMENTS, AND WHAT SOLUTIONS ARE AVAILABLE TO HANDLE CANCER TREATMENTS FINANCIALLY?

RACHEL: During my 40-plus years of life, I never felt more connected to Hashem than I did during the journey of fighting breast cancer. I focused on talking to Hashem directly and asking for the strength to face each day's challenges.

There are so many wonderful financial assistance programs out there. Women should reach out and ask their local Jewish community organizations, medical organizations, and others. Sharsheret, for example, provides financial assistance to women for treatments that are not typically covered by insurance, such as cold capping, tattooing, wigs, and certain yoga classes.

SHARI: Faith was what kept me going throughout. When I was afraid, miserable, and even angry, I never felt alone in the world or alone in my struggle to stay alive. This was a very deep comfort to me.

I was very lucky that I was able to keep working during this time, as was my husband. I know that this is often the exception, and that a serious disease can easily bankrupt a family. Patients and/or their partners lose time from work, and this alone can destroy a business or cause one to lose a job. Cancer can also be very expensive. There are many ancillary, non-medical costs that arise, such as the need for extra childcare, household help, transportation, etc.

I noticed this while I was sick and couldn't imagine how one coped with the fear of financial ruin on top of all the other fears. I researched and saw that other countries had special charities to support vulnerable women with breast cancer, but that Israel lacked one. In August 2011, I founded Israel's first and still only breast cancer emergency relief fund, The Lemonade Fund, to serve this need: to alleviate financial stress for Israeli citizens in active treatment so they can focus on recovery.

AFTER TREATMENT ENDED, HOW DID YOU BEGIN REBUILDING YOUR LIFE, AND WHAT DID HEALING LOOK LIKE FOR YOU BEYOND THE PHYSICAL ASPECT?

SHARI: It took me a while to get used to life again, but caring for my family, my architecture practice, and developing The Lemonade Fund kept me busy. Life goes on, and I was extremely grateful to be alive and busy with such good things.

I did learn to appreciate life in a new way, which was a gift. I wouldn't wish cancer on anyone, but we don't realize how easily we take life for granted. I live with a different level of gratitude now, and that's lovely.

RACHEL: After chemo and my second (reconstruction) surgery were completed, I made a decision to focus solely on my family's needs for the next year rather than the needs of the community or volunteer organizations. I needed to make up for lost time and to reassure them that I was able to return to being "mommy" like they remembered. Being able to return fully to my role as a mother and wife gave me great joy and comfort.

FEAR OF RECURRENCE IS SOMETHING MANY WOMEN STRUGGLE WITH. HOW DO YOU PERSONALLY COPE WITH THAT FEAR, AND WHAT WOULD YOU SAY TO SOMEONE LIVING WITH ONGOING UNCERTAINTY?

RACHEL: I have fear every day that a recurrence could, G-d forbid, occur. I personally know several women who have tragically faced difficult recurrences. But I have made a conscious decision not to let that fear consume me or overtake me. Instead, I look at each day as a new opportunity to live life to the fullest and appreciate each and every day and moment for what it is. I focus on the blessings I have been given, including the ability to live each day following my battle with breast cancer. Importantly, we are fortunate to live in a time when there are new medical treatments and advancements every day in many areas, including breast cancer.

SHARI: There is not much to say that can totally reassure anyone who has had breast cancer, as recurrence is a real possibility. I would say that some things are within our control, such as maintaining a healthy lifestyle, complying with medical advice, and being screened regularly. Treatments are always improving, and that is hopeful for all of us.

FOR WOMEN WHO ARE CURRENTLY HEALTHY, WHAT IS ONE HEALTH HABIT, CHECKUP, OR AWARENESS PRACTICE YOU WISH MORE WOMEN WOULD PRIORITIZE?

SHARI: Don't miss your yearly checkup or mammogram.

RACHEL: Beyond going to the doctor regularly, staying on top of your health treatments and screenings, and getting mammograms at the earliest recommended times, I would suggest that women prioritize their physical health with proper diet and exercise.

Through your involvement with The Lemonade Fund and Sharsheret, what do you see helps women in cancer treatment the most, what are the most common questions they ask, and what question would you like to ask each other as survivor to survivor?

RACHEL: In my personal and communal experience, women being able to talk to other women about their own experiences makes a tremendous difference. Common questions include

those around prophylactic surgical treatments, cold capping, and what symptoms and side effects to expect from chemotherapy and radiation. Having other women who have gone through the same experience to talk through these questions provides reassurance, comfort, and support. In this regard, one of Sharsheret's main offerings is peer-to-peer counseling and consultation for women, by women who have gone through breast and ovarian cancer.

SHARI: The Lemonade Fund does not deal with medical questions; we are not medical professionals. What we do help with is the potential financial impact of having cancer. No woman should have to miss treatment due to economic fears. "How will I feed my family and pay the rent if I have to miss work due to this illness?" is one of the first questions hospital social workers hear from the newly diagnosed.

All women should have equal access to treatment regardless of their socioeconomic status. Before we give women support groups, we need to give them reassurance that they can survive financially through that first year of treatment. The Lemonade Fund is now active in all Israeli hospitals and is a safety net, thanks to generous donors worldwide.

SHARI: Rachel, would you like to come visit me in Israel? I would love to host you!

RACHEL: I would love the opportunity to meet you, learn more about your organization, and help advance its goals and impact by getting involved and spreading the word.

Shari Mendes is the founder of The Israel Lemonade Fund, Israel's first and only breast cancer emergency relief fund. An architect originally from New Jersey, Shari and her husband made *Aliyah* with their four children in 2003. Her experience surviving breast cancer inspired her to create The Lemonade Fund in 2011, turning her personal challenge into a source of hope for others, making lemons into lemonade.

🌐 lemonadefund.org
▶ lsharimendes@lemonadefund.org

Rachel Silverman is a Chicago native, wife, mother of four, and community volunteer. She serves on the advisory committee of Sharsheret's Midwest Chapter and has held leadership roles with NILI, United Bikur Cholim of Chicago, and the Midwest Refuah Health Center. A breast cancer survivor, she is passionate about supporting women and families facing health challenges.

🌐 sharsheret.org
▶ rachsilverman1@gmail.com

Designing a Home That Supports Your Life

BY: CHANA LANDAU

We talk about homes all the time, how they look, how big they are, how much work they need, but we do not often talk about how they feel to live in. And yet, that feeling shapes our days more than we realize. Home is where we begin and end each day, where we host and retreat, where routines take hold and traditions find their place. Designing it thoughtfully is not about style or status. It is about care.

Over the years, I have learned that the homes people are happiest in are rarely the most dramatic. They are the ones that understand their owners. They reflect real rhythms, real needs, and real life. A well-designed home supports you without demanding attention.

One of the most important shifts I encourage is to start with life, not layout. Before choosing colors or furniture, it is worth pausing to notice how your days actually unfold. What makes mornings feel rushed? Where does clutter naturally collect? Where do people gravitate without being told? These small observations reveal far more than any visual inspiration ever could. When a home is shaped around who you truly are, rather than who you think you should be, it immediately feels calmer.

Space itself is not just about square meters. It is about intention. A room without a clear role often becomes a source of frustration, no matter how beautiful it looks. One practical approach is to make sure every area answers a simple question. What happens here most often? Even in an open plan, defining subtle zones through lighting, furniture placement, or a change in texture can bring a sense of order without closing anything off. Clarity creates ease, and ease changes how a home feels.

There is a particular comfort in a home that flows well. You sense it when you walk in. Nothing blocks your path. Nothing feels awkward or forced. This does not require minimalism, nor does it require abundance. It requires restraint. One useful rule I often share is this: if a piece does not serve daily life or bring genuine pleasure, it may simply be taking up emotional space.

In many Jewish homes, the kitchen or dining area naturally becomes the heart. This is where conversations linger, where guests drift in, where weekday life and Shabbat preparations overlap. Designing this space to be welcoming rather than impressive makes a meaningful difference. Comfortable seating matters more than matching chairs. Durable surfaces matter more than delicate ones. Lighting, often overlooked, can transform the entire mood. A balance of soft ambient light and focused task lighting allows the space to adapt easily from busy mornings to unhurried evenings.

Materials play a quiet but powerful role in how a home lives. Some finishes age gracefully, growing warmer with time, while others constantly demand attention. Choosing materials that are forgiving, easy to clean, pleasant to touch, and visually calm creates a sense of relief. One practical tip is to reserve more delicate materials for lower use areas and allow hardworking spaces to be just that, hardworking. A home that does not feel fragile is far more inviting.

I often hear women worry that they must choose between beauty and practicality. In reality, the most beautiful homes are

ART BY CHANA RACHEL GAFFIN

usually the ones that work best. A drawer that opens smoothly, a closet that actually fits what you own, or a counter with enough space to prepare a meal without juggling, brings a quiet satisfaction that decorative elements alone never can. When daily life feels easier, the home naturally feels more beautiful.

This becomes especially true during times of transition. Whether moving between countries, settling into a new environment, or redefining what home means at a certain stage of life, familiar elements offer grounding. Repeating a color you love, bringing along a beloved piece of furniture, or recreating a layout that once worked well can provide continuity even when everything else feels new. Home, in that sense, becomes an anchor.

Just as important is leaving room for meaning. Not every wall needs to be filled, and not every surface needs an object. When a home is visually crowded, the things that matter most are easily lost. Allowing for empty space gives weight to what remains. A cherished book, a meaningful piece, or a family heirloom does not need to compete. It needs room to breathe.

Perhaps the most comforting thought of all is that a home is never truly finished. It evolves as we do. Furniture moves. Our needs change. Life expands and contracts. A well considered home allows for that movement without losing its balance. It offers structure without rigidity and warmth without clutter.

In the end, a thoughtfully designed home feels generous. Generous in how it holds your day. Generous in how it welcomes others. Generous in how it allows life to unfold without constant friction. It does not strive for perfection or presentation. It simply supports you, so you can focus less on managing your surroundings and more on living within them. That is the essence of a home that truly works. It feels like it is on your side.

Chana Landau, originally from Monsey, NY, is a mother of seven and an interior designer. After making *Aliyah* and building a life fluent in both language and culture, she helps Anglo families create a home that feels familiar, functional, and truly theirs. Chana guides her clients through every decision for a calm, stress free design experience.

chanalandau.com

chana22806@gmail.com

Less Stuff, Easier Pesach

BY: ELLIE AZERAD

I had the bins.
The baskets.
The labels.
The systems.

And yet, somehow, I was always reorganizing.

I'll never forget my epiphany a couple of years ago.

I was standing in my playroom. Again. Reorganizing toys I had already reorganized three times that week. And suddenly, it hit me.

This is insane.

No system in the world can fix this.

The problem wasn't how things were organized.

The problem was that I had too much stuff.
So I did something drastic.

I grabbed duffel bags and filled them with about 90 percent of the toys in that room. And then something amazing happened.

I never had to organize that playroom again.
Not the next week.
Not the next year.
Not ever.

I used this approach in other areas of my home and my life. That moment was the beginning of what I call "Frum Minimalism".

And in this article, I want to show you how having less stuff, clearer priorities, and simpler planning can completely change the way you experience *Pesach* prep.

1: KNOW WHAT PESACH ACTUALLY IS

This is the most important step.

We need to remember that there is a huge difference between the *halachic* obligation of removing *chametz* from our homes and spring cleaning.

Spring cleaning is a bonus.
It's nice.
A lot of women enjoy it. I enjoy it too.
But it is not the *mitzvah*.

The *mitzvah* is simple: remove *chametz* from your home.

I often joke that when it comes to *Pesach* cleaning, there are two types of women. The ones who brag about how early they started and how hard they're working. And the ones who cry, complain, and count the days until it's over.

But if we focus on the actual obligation, *Pesach* cleaning becomes far more manageable. Maybe not effortless, but it should not feel like slavery.

Most of what we do under the banner of "*Pesach* cleaning" is actually spring cleaning.

Optional.
Nice.
But not the *mitzvah*.

2: THE IMPORTANCE OF NO CLUTTER

Once we understand the basics, if you have the capacity to do more, decluttering is where *Pesach* prep becomes dramatically easier.

Clutter raises cortisol, the stress hormone. The more stuff we have, the more stressed we feel. No wonder so many women feel overwhelmed, snappy, exhausted, and done.

We are surrounded by stuff all the time. Even if it looks neat. Even if it's in bins. Even if it's labeled.

If you are unsure what to get rid of, ask yourself a simple question. Do I need it, use it, or love it?

If that still feels unclear, ask yourself whether you already own something that does the same job. Ask if you own duplicates or triples. And ask yourself honestly, if this disappeared tomorrow, would I replace it immediately or manage without it?

Decluttering is one of the most effective forms of *Pesach* prep you can do.

3: WORKING BACKWARD

Working backward is one of my favorite planning tools. I use it for all major life events and teach it regularly.

Start with the due date and write it at the top of a page. Then break everything down and work backward.

Pesach begins on the night of the 15th of *Nissan*. By that night, everything must be done.

Write your finish line clearly.

By *Pesach* night, the house is *chametz* free. The house is clean. You and your children have *Yom Tov* clothing. Food is ready. The table is set.

Now ask one question only. What needs to happen right before this?

Take one item and walk it backward.

When clutter sits on a surface, cleaning becomes a three step process. You move the items, clean the surface, and then put everything back. That is exhausting.

When there is no clutter, you clean once. Done.

Now think about *Pesach*.

Less stuff means fewer drawers to empty, fewer shelves to wipe, and fewer piles to deal with. *Pesach* cleaning becomes faster simply because there is less to clean.

If food must be ready, the kitchen must be koshered.

If the kitchen must be koshered, it must be cleaned.

If it must be cleaned, cabinets must be cleared.

If cabinets must be cleared, decisions must be made.

If food must be cooked, a menu is needed.

If a menu is needed, ingredients must be purchased.

If ingredients are needed, shopping must happen first.

You keep going backward one step at a time.

Do not think about everything at once. You are only answering one question. What comes right before this?

Once you have your list, add dates and time estimates next to each task. Then put them into your calendar. Your calendar should tell you what you are doing, when you are doing it, and that everything will be done on time.

A FEW IMPORTANT REMINDERS

- *Pesach* cleaning does not mean cleaning your ceilings with a toothbrush.

- The *mitzvah* is removing *chametz*.
  Not scrubbing behind the washing machine.
  Not washing ceilings.
  Not cleaning places food never goes.
  Those things can be nice. They can be satisfying. But they are not the *mitzvah*.

- There is a well-known saying often attributed to the Lubavitcher Rebbe: "Dust is not *chametz*, and children are not the *Korban Pesach*."

- Read that again.

- And finally, get help. Paid help. Cleaning help. Family help. Friend help.

Anything you do for *Yom Tov* is free. *Hashem* pays you back.

Ellie (Elisheva) Azerad is the creator of *Frum Minimalism*, where she helps women create lasting order at home and in life. With warmth, honesty, and practical tools, she goes beyond tidy spaces to help you let go of what no longer serves you, reclaim clarity, and make room for what truly matters.

🌐 **frumminimalism.com**

How to Stay Me in Marriage

BY: REBBETZIN BAT CHEN GROSSMAN

Pesach isn't about nostalgia. It's about freedom. And freedom doesn't start with changing your circumstances. It starts when you stop accepting limitations you slowly made peace with and begin to question what you assumed couldn't change.

A lot of women carry a quiet thought they don't say out loud: "I'm not who I used to be. I lost myself somewhere along the way." The instinct is to want to go back. "I wish I could get back to myself!" But going back isn't the answer. Life moves forward. When we fight that, it turns into exhaustion, resentment, and that yucky feeling of being stuck.

From that place, you ask for help. You bring *Hashem* into the picture in a grounded way. You can say, this is what matters to me, this is what I feel called to, but I do not know how. Please guide me.

Then you listen. We were taught how to ask, but not how to listen. A rabbi once told me something that changed how I see everything. "*Hashem* wants what is. If He did not want it, it would not be." Reality itself often carries the answer. A conversation. Timing. A sentence your husband says unexpectedly. Sometimes a yes comes through another person. Sometimes a no is not rejection, but redirection.

The key is paying attention. Answers are often missed because we rush past them.

The final step is integration. If you do not pause and acknowledge what shifted, you end up exhausted, always growing but never resting. Integration looks like thanking *Hashem*, noticing what changed, and allowing your nervous system to learn that peace and clarity are allowed.

You were never meant to return to who you were. You are meant to grow into who you're becoming now. The woman you once were didn't disappear. She was exactly where she needed to be in order to show you what's possible. The real question isn't how do I get her back, but how do I step into the next version of myself without losing myself again.

This question shows up powerfully in marriage. In the beginning, there is excitement and sweetness. You want to make your husband happy. You are willing to give up on yourself because it feels devoted and loving. Then one day you wake up and realize, I lost myself. I feel erased. I do not know where I am anymore.

Then life adds layers. Children. Responsibilities. Sleep deprivation. A million roles. Instead of growth, it can feel like repetition, day after day.

Let me say this clearly. You are not the problem. This is normal.

Raising young children is the most important work you will ever do, and also the hardest. I once had a neighbor who told young mothers, "you are doing holy work, and I am proud of you." Every time she said it, I wanted to cry. So many women are carrying something heavy, yet everyone makes it look so easy, "So why is this so hard for me?".

It's hard because it's hard. It's the most valuable thing you'll ever do! And it is also holy.

Here's the deal: We were created limited. *Hashem* is limitless. When a limited human connects to a limitless G-d, she experiences a different kind of freedom. Not because she suddenly has special powers, but because she stops carrying everything alone. We were made limited so we would seek *Hashem* and cling to Him. When that connection deepens, flow returns. Doors open. You can breathe again. You are no longer holding it all alone!

Every marriage develops patterns. The first challenge is noticing them. The second is believing they can change. Many couples know the script. I say something. He reacts. I get hurt. I get angry. He gets angrier. We stop talking. Something explodes. Then we make up and pretend it did not happen, while our bodies quietly keep score. That loop can feel permanent.

But patterns can be cracked.

One of the core frameworks I teach is a simple process for restoring flow. It begins with connecting to yourself. You cannot shift anything until you are honest about what truly matters to you, not what you should want and not what looks right from the outside. Many women live for years on "should," and then realize they are living for everyone else.

Connection does not need to be dramatic. It can take five minutes. A walk while talking to *Hashem*. Writing a few honest lines. Sitting quietly. Anything that softens the noise so you can hear your inner voice. Silence can feel uncomfortable, but silence is where truth lives.

Holding space does not mean erasing yourself to keep the peace. Many women put their dreams on hold because marriage comes first, children come first, and everyone needs them more. They wait for a future season when there will finally be room to breathe.

But ignoring a real calling dims you, and what you were meant to bring into the world.

Aligned action does not mean abandoning your family. It means taking even one small step toward what fills you and serves *Hashem*. When you do, you show up more alive. Your children learn what is possible. And you can truly hold space for your husband's dreams because you are no longer collapsing your own.

Boundaries are part of staying yourself in marriage. Many women sense where a line should be, but when it is crossed, they shrink it, explain it away, or move it to keep the peace. Over time, this creates confusion, for everyone, including ourselves. The weakest boundary is the one we do not hold. Real boundaries come from clarity about what truly matters to YOU, then asking *Hashem* for strength and trusting your intuition when something feels off. This is not about control. It is about self-respect, practiced over time.

Renewal works the same way. It is not about getting it right once and being done. It is about returning to yourself again and again. Sometimes life knocks you down and it feels like all your growth disappeared. But growth is rarely erased. More often, it is revisited from a deeper place, with more honesty, humility, and strength than before.

Hashem is not trying to break you when He pushes you. He is guiding you toward who you are meant to become and helping you reframe how you see yourself and what you believe about yourself. Challenges are not punishments. They are invitations into who you can become next.

This *Pesach*, remember: you are not stuck. Patterns are not prison. Loops are not destiny. If you believe you are here for a reason, you will find it. And if you connect to yourself, invite *Hashem* in, listen, and integrate what you receive, freedom will become something you live, not just something you talk about.

You are so awesome. And you are not alone.

Rebbetzin Bat-Chen Grossman is the creator of The CALM Method™, a practical framework that integrates *Hashem* into daily life, marriage, and business. She lives in Israel with her husband, Rabbi Avi Grossman, and their eight children. Her mission is to help women build loving families while growing meaningful, aligned work.

- connectedforreal.com
- connectedforreal.com/guide
- advice@connectedforreal.com

The Four Sons
at Our Parenting Table

BY: TZIPORAH WAYNE, M.ED

Most of us did not grow up imagining that parenting would feel quite this intense. We love our children deeply, and yet we find ourselves asking questions no one prepared us for. How do I stay calm when everything feels urgent? How do I set boundaries without becoming harsh? How do I parent differently than I was parented when I do not always have the tools? How do I focus on seeing what is good when it is so easy to see what is not?

Pesach reminds us that children do not all ask in the same way. Some question openly, some challenge, some stay quiet, and some do not yet know how to ask at all. The wisdom of the Four Sons is not about labels. It is about responsiveness. It teaches us that connection begins when we learn how to listen beneath behavior and respond to the child in front of us, in this moment. Parenting asks the same of us every day.

At the heart of these questions is one shared desire: real connection, with our children and with ourselves.

Through my work with children and parents, my training in the Nurtured Heart Approach, and years of experience, I learned that connection does not come from being a perfect parent. It comes from learning how to see and communicate greatness, reducing unnecessary negativity, and holding clear, calm boundaries, even when this was not modeled for us growing up. These are skills that can be learned, one step at a time. I believe *Hashem* wants this growth for us.

Gentle Parenting and Being Too Soft

Where is the line?

Gentle parenting does not mean weak or permissive parenting. Kindness does not cancel authority.

Children feel safest when boundaries are clear, consistent, and calm. You can say, "No hitting" or "I will not let you hit," without yelling, threatening, or shaming. You can also acknowledge when your child is showing self-control, especially when you know how hard that moment is for them.

The *Torah* teaches us to educate a child according to their way. This requires an ayin tovah, training our eyes to notice what is good. This is how we grow greatness in our children and in ourselves.

Kindness is not the absence of limits. It is the tone and energy with which we hold them.

Cooperation Without Yelling or Bribing

In stressful moments, especially when siblings are melting down and everything feels urgent, our instinct is often to raise our voice or offer rewards. Yet cooperation grows when children feel seen, needed, and engaged, not managed.

Two inner shifts consistently make the biggest difference: holding hope and cultivating awareness.

Hope means holding a vision of your child's G-d-given strengths and abilities, even when things look messy in the moment. Awareness creates space to notice your own triggers and patterns. When we pause long enough to regulate ourselves first, our children borrow that calm. This is *gevurah*, inner strength and self-control.

Before correcting, slowing the process down can change everything. Naming what is going right builds connection:

"I see how hard you are trying."

"You are having a big moment and you are still listening."

Building cooperation and teamwork is far more enriching than yelling or bribing.

Is Punishment an Option

So many of us grew up with punishment as the only option. Punishment may stop behavior temporarily, but often at the cost of connection. It teaches children what not to do. They also need guidance, time, and space to learn what to do instead.

Clear consequences are different. Consequences are calm, predictable, and respectful. They are paired with teaching and repair. Boundaries held with calm consistency can be firm and still gentle.

Hashem gave us *halachos* for our benefit, to help us choose what is good and draw closer to Him. We are not struck down when we make mistakes. We are given space for *teshuvah* and forgiveness. Can we hold that same space for our children?

When a child talks back or is *chutzpadik*, it is often a sign of overwhelm, hunger, exhaustion, or disconnection. Our opportunity is to address the behavior clearly, without attacking the child's character.

Rabbi Ilan Feldman teaches, "If you want to raise a *mensch*, you need to be a *mensch*." If we want to teach respect, we must model it, even when we feel triggered. This is our *avodah*.

Bedtime, Teens, and Guilt

Transitions are hard, even for adults. Children are decompressing from their day and letting go of stimulation. A predictable bedtime routine helps. Even a few focused minutes of connection matter.

"It is bedtime now. I love you. I am here."

Teenagers bring a different stage. Over time, our role shifts from Director to Supervisor. Connection with teens grows through respect and curiosity, not coercion. *Pesach* invites us to release fear-based parenting and trust the process of growth.

Guilt is only helpful if it leads to growth, not self-criticism. Your children do not need perfection. They need genuine presence. A calm, grounded parent, even briefly, nourishes more than hours of distracted guilt.

Returning to Connection

Over time, the patterns I observed naturally formed language: **H**ope, **A**wareness, **P**ausing, choosing **P**ositivity and **P**ractice. The **Y** = Yes to Success— noticing and celebrating small victories and any progress in the right direction.

These ideas eventually came together in what I call the H.A.P.P.Y. Heart Framework, not as a formula, but as a reminder of what consistently brings families back to connection.

Parenting is not about getting it right. It is about returning to connection again and again. Like our relationship with *Hashem*, it is our hearts, not perfection, that matter most.

May this *Pesach* help us release what no longer serves us, see the goodness already present, and parent from freedom rather than fear.

P.S. Listen to Mordechai Shapiro's song "Trying My Best" as a heartfelt tefilla from parents to Hashem, and then again from our children's perspective.

Tziporah Wayne, M.Ed., is a Parenting Coach, founder of the Raising a Mensch Masterclass Series, and an Advanced Trainer of the Nurtured Heart Approach. She supports Jewish parents in raising a mensch with connection, compassion, and joy, grounded in Torah wisdom and belief in the greatness within every child and parent.

🌐 **myhappyheartcoach.com**
▶ **Newsletter: Happy Heart Families: Parenting with the *Parsha* – email to join.**
▶ **info@myhappyheartcoach.com**

BETWEEN MEMORY AND NOW:
Sheila the Centenarian

BY: CHAVA RACHEL SABAN

When the war in Israel began, I felt, like so many others, that I needed to do more to help my country. As a violinist, I looked for ways to bring joy through music, and so I began performing for groups of seniors. Someone at the *Beit Avot* told a friend about me, and this is how I met Granny Sheila.

61

Sheila—101 years old, *bli ayin hara*—lives with her caretaker in Jerusalem. When I say I receive far more from her than she receives from me, it's no exaggeration. Sheila was a dancer in her youth, and she loves to show off her tiny black leather ballet shoes, then the next pair—a bit bigger—and finally, her faded pink pointe shoes. "Now these are used only when the girl's body has matured," she tells me with pride.

On the day we met, she told me clearly that she's not musical—doesn't even like music—but loves rhythm. I thought, what am I doing here? I'm not a drummer! I almost called her daughter to say this was a mistake. But I began to play anyway.

I've been performing since I was four years old, but never in my life have I played for someone who becomes so entirely alive from the first note. Sheila sways, conducts me with her arms, pirouettes gently from her chair.

Sometimes she closes her eyes, and then—suddenly—our eyes meet and she smiles with all her being, as if drinking in every sound. Her joy feeds my music; I give more of myself and together we enter a timeless space beyond words. In those moments, there is no war, no worry about my soldier son or *parnassa*, no anxiety about how the *Geula* will unfold—only music, and the two of us inside it.

Before I play, we talk. About everything—world events, Jewish customs, her life in South Africa, antisemitism, and why the violin is a Jewish instrument. Her floor is often sprinkled with newspaper clippings, her table piled with articles that spark her curiosity. I once learned that when elders repeat themselves, we must let them. It's what they came into the world to say.

Sheila loves discussing what it means to be a Jew. "You see, anti-Judaism is bringing us together. You might not believe it—but I think antisemitism is actually a good thing. Call Him whatever you like—G-d, or Whomever—He's doing this," she says, circling a finger upward. "The more antisemitism there is, the more Jews stay together. The Jewish boy will marry a Jewish girl, there'll be *bar mitzvahs*, *brit milahs*, and we discover who we are. That's a very good thing."

She often reflects on her life in South Africa, raising a family with the ever-present worry that her sons would marry non-Jewish girls. She wasn't raised observant, but she met her husband on the way to a Jewish event in Johannesburg. "All the boys were together, and all the girls were together," she recalls, smiling. Apartheid South

Africa was a confusing place, but Sheila clung to her Jewish identity. "The blacks spoke all different languages—each from a different tribe. And our enemies today—they are also not united! But we have one *Torah*. The same prayers all over the world. The same *yomim tovim*. The same *Torah* portion every *Shabbat*."

Despite differences, she insists, the Jewish people are one. G-d is one. Am Yisrael is one.

One day, her children discovered *Bnei Akiva*—and that began an intergenerational journey of *teshuva*. The children began teaching their parents *Torah* and *mitzvot*. Eventually the family (except one daughter) emigrated to Israel. Now Sheila has numerous descendants—*bli ayin hara*!

There's much research about the power of music to awaken memory in the elderly. When I prepare playlists to accompany my violin for Sheila, I use a mix of *klezmer*, Yiddish songs, modern Israeli tunes, and "the moldy oldies." Her daughter Joanne once joined us as we listened to waltzes. "Do you remember the ballroom dancing, Mum?" she asked. Sheila smiled: yes, she remembers.

She remembers getting her driver's license at sixteen. She remembers giving birth to Joanne at forty. She remembers when Israel became a state, listening to the news on the radio. She remembers that my daughter had a baby last month. But she often doesn't remember whose *simcha* she attended last week or where she went for *Shabbos*. "Oh, I can't remember anything," she laughs. "And at my age, you don't think about the future. So what does that leave?"

It leaves the present—the full, luminous present moment, which is all that matters.

These visits have changed me. Every week I slow down and glimpse life through the eyes of a centenarian. I am privileged to share music and witness its power to heal, soothe, evoke feeling and memory. And yes—I am reminded that our time here is like a passing shadow. *Ad meah v'esrim*.

I asked Sheila her secret to a long life. She shrugged. "Genetics," she said. Proudly, she adds that she doesn't take any medications and has never had an operation. Often there's chocolate or cake on the table—she's no health fanatic. But after getting to know her, I suspect her longevity comes from her passionate love affair with G-d, the Jewish people, and the State of Israel. And she is exactly where she needs to be to keep going.

Chava Rachel Saban studied violin and literature at Yale University, and has played with several professional symphonies including the New Haven Sympony. Her life began anew in Israel where she raised a family, and released 7 CDs of original music. She teaches violin, is a section leader of Zmora Women's Orchestra and also plays for the elderly.
havarahel@yahoo.com

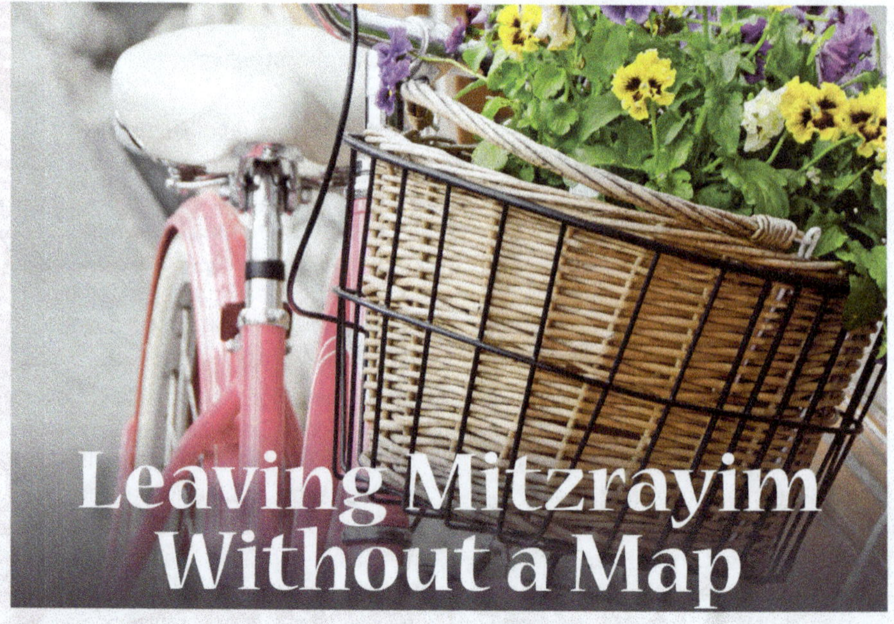

Leaving Mitzrayim Without a Map

BY: DANIELLE SHAI

Having blind faith in *Hashem* is trusting and knowing in His actions and His choices without a need for justification or explanation. It is an overwhelming sense of belief that He is working for our greater good, even when nothing makes sense yet.

I am not sharing this from a place of being higher or holier. Blind faith has been, and still is, a constant journey for me. Coming to a place where I can say that I truly trust *Hashem* is relatively new. It was not something I always believed in or felt like I always had.

For a long time, I felt like a victim of my own story.

Things happened throughout my life without explanation. I spent weeks, months, even years dwelling and overanalyzing situations, trying to understand why things happened the way they did. I needed answers before I could move forward.

A few months ago, I finished law school. This was something I worked so hard for. But when I reflect back, I realize it was not something I deeply questioned. I did not ask myself if this path was actually going to feed my soul. It simply unfolded, the way many things in life do.

After graduating, I started applying for jobs. When I tell you I applied to a thousand positions, I mean it. It was no after no after no. Doors closing before I could even open them. And all I could think was, why is this not working? I did everything right.

Around that same time, I went for a walk with my mom. And I felt this quiet inner voice saying, you are looking in the wrong place. You are doing the wrong thing. Is this what is going to feed your soul?

This does not mean I will never be a lawyer. That passion still exists. But I felt a calling for something different. A desire to share simple *emunah* and create connection.

If I had not gotten all those "no" answers and had gone straight into a legal role, I do not know if this space would exist. That was my personal proof of why blind faith matters and why we are asked to trust *Hashem*'s plan even when we do not understand it.

Pesach teaches us this truth so clearly. First we do, and only later do we understand. Leaving *Mitzrayim* was not about clarity. It was about movement.

So what does blind faith look like in daily life?

For me, it starts with surrender. When you completely surrender to *Hashem* and put your trust in His plan, I cannot even describe the relief that comes over you. It does not happen in one day. It is a gradual process, learning to trust Him moment by moment.

I used to need everything planned. I needed to control, anticipate, and predict. I am not that person anymore, and the freedom in that is everything.

I do not take things personally anymore. If something does not go the way I thought it would, I trust that it is for a reason I cannot yet see. Rejection stopped feeling like failure. I am also no longer in competition with time. That voice of "I should be further by now" no longer runs my life. I know everything is unfolding in divine timing.

I have also learned to trust when things are removed from my life. There were situations that were forcibly taken away because I was not willing to remove myself from them. Now I feel more in tune with what is for me and what is not.

From this place, eight truths became clear to me.

FIRST, the more you give, the more you receive. This is not only physical, but spiritual and emotional. Giving expands your vessel. Withholding shrinks it.

SECOND, whatever you judge, you will ultimately experience. Judgment tunes

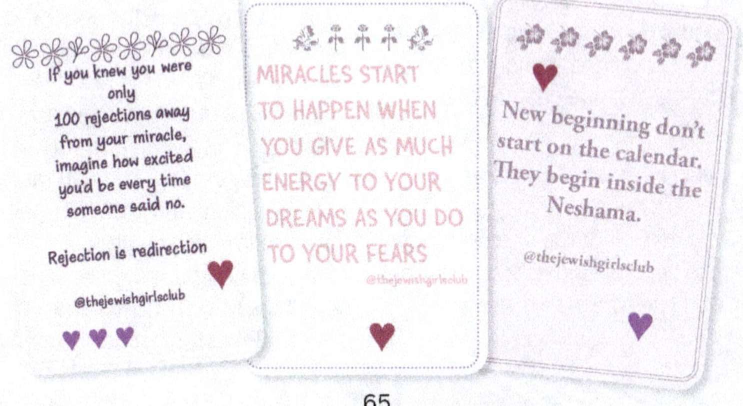

SECOND, whatever you judge, you will ultimately experience. Judgment tunes us into harshness and brings it back into our lives.

THIRD, *Hashem* works through you when your desires align with His purpose. When something is meant to happen, it unfolds in a way that feels undeniably guided.

FOURTH, gratitude is the bridge between you and what could be. Gratitude expands your vessel and opens the channel for what is already forming.

FIFTH, if you do not spend time getting to know yourself, you will absorb everyone else's definition of who you are. Becoming your own best friend creates stability no one can shake.

SIXTH, you are allowed to begin again as many times as it takes. You have not missed your moment.

SEVENTH, when you feel scared, that is often the moment to jump. Fear does not mean something is wrong.

EIGHTH, comfort is the enemy of growth. The soul did not come into this world for ease. It came for refinement and elevation.

Blind faith does not mean pretending pain is good. You are allowed to feel sadness, disappointment and grief, while knowing this is just one chapter of a bigger story.

I practice faith in the smallest moments. Traffic. Delays. Disruptions. Maybe the slow driver saved my life. Maybe my coffee was not meant to be sweet today. I do not let the external world determine my inner world.

My mom always told me, do not let the outside determine your inside. If you place your happiness in other people's hands, you will always be at their mercy. When you place your trust in *Hashem's* hands, you are no longer dependent on circumstances.

Our story has already been written. Our purpose is already known by the Creator. There is no such thing as a wrong turn.

If you are standing at a crossroads, afraid to choose left or right, this is your sign.

Just turn.

Trust that *Hashem* will guide the rest.

When I let go of the need to know why, how, and when, I felt free.

And that is the freedom I want every woman to experience.

Danielle Shai is the founder of The Jewish Girls Club podcast and community. She inspires modern Jewish women to awaken the timeless wisdom of Judaism within their DNA, blending ancient truth with contemporary life. Through media, conversation, and creativity, she helps women live with clarity, confidence, faith, and purpose—daily, globally.

The Jewish Girls Club
thejewishgirlsclub@gmail.com

I Wanted Judaism to Feel Real

BY: LIORA HARUNI

There are moments in life when you stop and ask yourself what you are really living for. Not what you do, not what you produce, but what you are carrying inside. *Pesach* always brings me to that place. It asks questions. It asks where we come from, what we are holding onto, and what we are passing on. Quietly but firmly, it asks what kind of Jewish life we are choosing to live.

I know this question well.

I did not come to Israel to live Judaism from the outside. I came because I wanted Judaism to be life itself. I wanted *Pesach* to be something my body remembers, not just my mind. I wanted *Sukkot* to be built and felt, not explained. I wanted my children to grow up inside Jewish time, Jewish rhythm, Jewish responsibility.

I grew up in Belgium in a Modern Orthodox family, but outside of my home I often felt alone in my observance. I was the only one keeping *Shabbat*, the only one eating kosher. Judaism existed, but it felt fragile, almost theoretical. I knew very early on that I did not want to raise a family like that. I wanted Jewish life to be lived fully, openly, and with confidence.

That longing is what led me to make *Aliyah*.

I arrived in Israel on *Erev Yom Kippur*. I remember the exhaustion, the fear, and the certainty. I went straight to the *Kotel*. I did not question the decision. I knew I was home.

Creation has always been part of who I am, but never as decoration. For more than twenty years, I taught mosaic. Women came to my classes convinced they were not creative. They told me they had two left hands. And then something would shift. At the end of a workshop, a woman would step back, look at what she had made, and say with surprise, "I

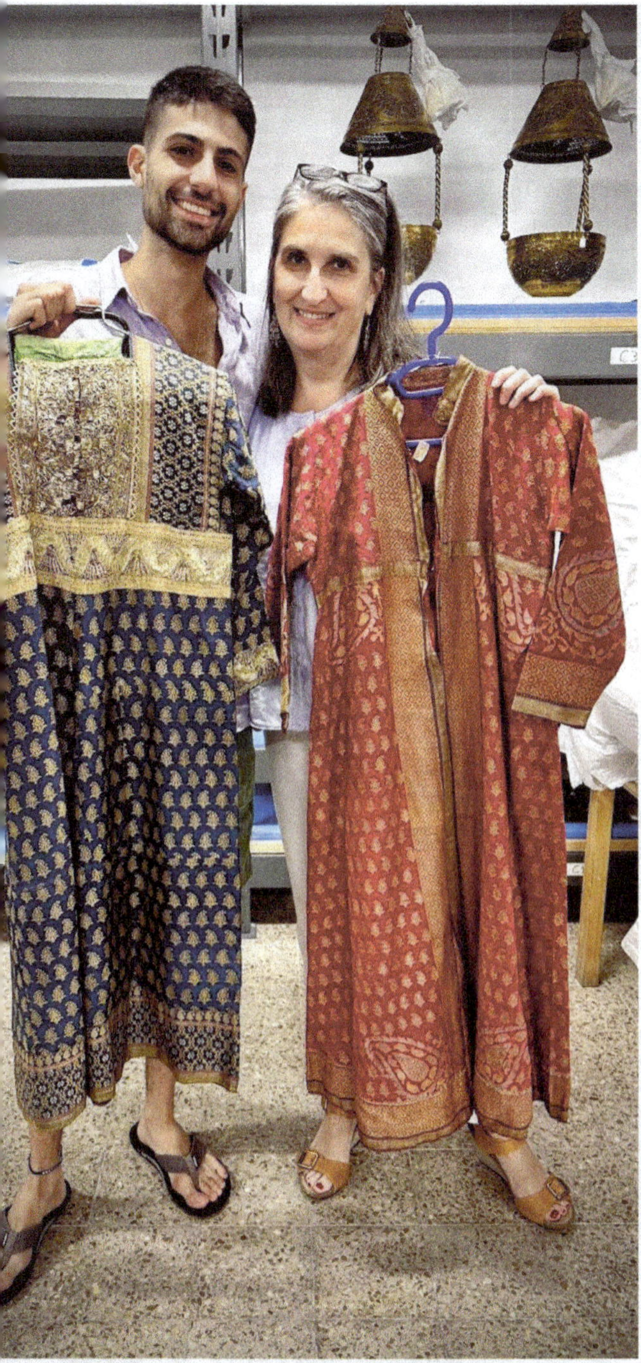

PHOTO COURTESY OF LIORA HARUNI

cannot believe I created something so beautiful."

That moment was magical for me. It gave me more fulfillment than any commission I ever received. I created mosaics for wealthy homes and important spaces, even for people everyone knows. But it felt like nothing compared to allowing women to discover their own creative potential. That felt meaningful. Almost sacred.

After many years of helping others create, I felt a subtle change. When I reached fifty, I knew it was time to create myself again. Not because I wanted attention, and not because the world needed more objects. The world is already full. Too full. What it lacks is meaning.

I did not want to create clutter. I wanted to create something that carries weight.

I found myself looking closely at the *Shabbat* table. Not as an object, but as a reflection of values. I reflected on the beauty of a *Hiddur*

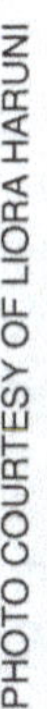

Mitzvah. I noticed how much care is given to the *kiddush* cup, how carefully it is chosen, while the challah cover is often secondary. For me, this felt symbolic. The *challot* represent the woman's presence at the table. The hours of preparation. The hosting. The love that holds everything together and is rarely named.

I wanted to give dignity to that.

I wanted to treat the *challah* cover the way we treat jewelry. Not as decoration, but as something that elevates a moment. Just as a woman puts on a piece of jewelry to honor an occasion, I wanted something on the table that says: this moment matters, and so does the woman who created it. The inspiration for the details comes from antique Judaica, for example *ketubot*, where beauty and meaning are inseparable.

The technique I was drawn to is called *zardozi*, a Persian embroidery technique made with metallic threads. I first encountered it in India. When I began researching its history, something very strong happened inside me. I learned that the technique arrived in India from Persia about 150 years ago. Immediately, I felt this could not be a coincidence. Persian Jews fled pogroms and made that exact journey.

This was not abstract history. It was my husband's family's story.

As I researched further and spoke with experts, I learned that Jews were often embroiderers for kings. Within the Jewish community, they created ceremonial garments, household objects, and Jewish wedding dresses, which at the time were not white, often using leftover precious threads from commissioned work. In periods when Jews were forbidden from many professions, embroidery became a means of survival, continuity, and memory.

Then it became deeply personal.

My husband's grandmother fled Persia at the age of twenty-six, alone with four small children. She had married at eleven as a form of protection. Jews blended outwardly into the surrounding population, much like the Marranos. Her husband was already in Mumbai. To escape safely, she said she was traveling on the Hajj. She took very little with her. Only a few bundles and her wedding dress.

That dress survived everything. Persia. India. Israel. England. And finally Israel again. Years later, it was donated to the ANU Museum.

When my son and I began working together, I suggested we go to see the dress. Standing in front of it, we realized something that left us silent. The embroidery was made using the exact same threads and the same technique I use today. A hundred-year-old dress, speaking the same language of gold and thread.

At that moment, I understood that this was not only a family story. It was the story of Jewish continuity itself.

Strength has always come to me through women. My maternal grandmother survived the Lodz Ghetto, Auschwitz, Bergen Belsen, and the death marches. After the war, she rebuilt her life in Paris.

She was an artist. She embroidered. She painted. I believe art saved her. To survive such darkness, you must be able to see beauty. Beauty gives you a reason to continue.

On both sides of my family, the *Shoah* erased almost everyone. My father was an orphan. I live with the absence of extended family every day. That absence is one of the reasons building a life in Israel feels so meaningful to me. It is a declaration that the story did not end.

I believe Judaism is carried by women. Through love. Through care. Through the silent, daily gestures no one applauds. That belief is why I chose the name Malqeta for my brand—Aramaic for queen…the *Shabbat* Queen. I wanted to draw attention to the woman, to say that we are all queens—each one of us. Married or not, mothers or not—every woman.

Women give endlessly, often placing themselves last. I know this well. My hope is simple. That something small can return something large. Presence. Dignity. Worth.

My son finished his army service just as we were meant to travel together. The suitcase was packed. Then October came. He was called back into reserve duty. Before leaving, he told me, "Mama, the person who leaves this house will not be the same person who comes back."

He lost friends. We lived with uncertainty. And still, life continued. I held on through teaching, through creating, and through being surrounded by women living the same fear.

Working together transformed our relationship. What began as observation grew into trust and a true partnership. I am deeply proud of my son—of his dedication to protecting our home and our community, and of the same care he brings to creating Judaica for Jewish families. Judaica is a symbol of continuity, carrying meaning from one generation to the next.

With *Hashem's* guidance and thanks to Michal Herzog, my work found its way to the President's Residence, under Isaac Herzog. Knowing it may help elevate the *Shabbat* tables of our leaders brings me a deep sense of *nachat*.

As *Pesach* approaches, a time of questions, memory, and transmission, I look at my children and understand what freedom means to me. They were born here. The chain continues.

That is my answer.

Liora Haruni is a mosaic artist and educator living in Israel since 1993. Born in Brussels, she has taught and created for over 30 years. She is the founder of Malqeta, luxury Judaica inspired by Jewish history, women's legacy, and meaningful ritual.

lioraharuni@gmail.com

malqeta.com

@malqeta

Hair Covering, Freedom, and Choosing Purpose

BY: MEIRAV AFTALION

I didn't grow up religious.

I grew up traditional, Jewish, connected, but not observant. At a certain point in my life, I let go of almost everything. I wasn't keeping *mitzvot*. I wasn't searching either. I was simply living.

And then, about nine years ago, something unexpected happened.

I had a dream.

It wasn't dramatic, but when I woke up, I felt something I had never felt before. A deep urge to pray. Not for a moment, not for a reason. I wanted a connection. I wanted truth.

People around me told me to let it go. "It's just a dream," they said. But my sister, who was already religious, suggested I come to a class in Israel. I went, and something inside me opened. I fell in love. Two months later, I became religious. A year after that, I was married.

Everything happened very fast.

Soon after my wedding, I moved to Los Angeles. Suddenly, I found myself far from everything that grounded me. My family was in Israel. My *rabbanit* was in Israel. My spiritual foundation was in Israel. I was living in L.A., but my heart wasn't there.

I cried a lot. I felt lonely. COVID only intensified those feelings. Like many people, I found myself asking, what am I doing here? What is my purpose?

At some point, I realized I couldn't keep waiting for life to start. I couldn't sit and wait to return to Israel while doing nothing with my life. I needed to live fully where I was.

That's when hair covering became central to my journey.

When my husband and I first spoke about marriage, one of the first questions he asked me was whether I planned to cover my hair. For me, the answer was obvious. I didn't even know there was another option.

I grew up knowing only one model, women who covered their hair with a *mitpachat*. Mostly *Chassidic* women. That was all I knew. When I arrived in L.A., I was shocked to discover how few young women were covering their hair, and how sensitive and confusing the topic felt for so many.

There were so many voices. So many opinions. So much pressure. Different styles, different levels, different expectations. It felt overwhelming.

And if I'm honest, I had to grow.

I had to learn that hair covering is not one size fits all. I had to unlearn judgment and replace it with curiosity.

I began researching. Learning. Speaking to women. Trying different styles. I experimented with tying techniques, heights, fabrics, and colors. I tried covering more, covering less, adjusting depending on the day. I wasn't looking for perfection. I was looking for truth. Something that felt authentic, dignified, and realistic for my life.

I'm a very logical person. Even if something is "allowed," I need to feel at peace with it internally. I needed my *mitzvah* to feel aligned, not forced.

What guided me most was how it felt.

When something felt heavy, I didn't quit. I adjusted. When something felt beautiful and natural, I stayed with it. Confidence, I learned, doesn't come from copying others, but from finding what truly works for you.

Covering my hair made me stand out in L.A. But instead of shrinking, I felt proud. Women would stop me and ask how I tied my *mitpachat*, how I made it look simple and effortless. I realized how many women wanted to take a step forward, but they just didn't want pressure.

My grandmother was always in the back of my mind. She was the only woman in my family who covered her hair, not out of ideology, but because it felt right to her. Even at the end of her life, she insisted on covering her head, and that quiet dignity stayed with me.

For me, hair covering is not about control. It's about balance.

I don't believe in "anything goes." I believe boundaries create safety. They help us build homes. They help us build marriages. They help us hold both freedom and structure at the same time.

Outside, I cover my hair. Inside my home, I feel free. That balance protects something precious.

Our hair holds power. Covering it isn't about hiding. It's about choosing.

Choosing where and with whom we express that power.

Pesach speaks deeply to me in this way.

True freedom isn't comfort. It isn't doing whatever we want. Many people stayed in *Mitzrayim* because they were comfortable there. Growth requires movement. Discomfort. Courage.

Covering my hair isn't always easy. Styling takes thought. Some days it works, some days it doesn't. But that process itself is part of the freedom, choosing intention over autopilot, choosing to be an *eved Hashem*, (servant of *Hashem*).

There was also a very painful period in my life when this *mitzvah* took on an even deeper meaning.

After three miscarriages in a row, I felt devastated and heartbroken. In that place of loss, I needed something steady—something I could hold onto. That was the push I needed to open my mitpachot business, and my work became part of how I healed my soul. It gave me purpose, structure, and a way to transform pain into creation.

Naming my brand after my grandmother was not a branding decision, but a personal one. It keeps me connected to this mitzvah and honors her memory in the most meaningful way.

I didn't want to tell women what they should do. I wanted to show them how it can be done. Practically. Simply. Beautifully. In a way that feels achievable.

Hair covering doesn't have to feel heavy or intimidating. It can be expressive, creative, and empowering. Sometimes all a woman needs is to see one simple option and think, "Oh, I can do that."

This isn't about selling fabric. It's about confidence, dignity, and connection. To *mitzvah*. To heritage. To ourselves. To *Hashem*.

At the end of the day, it's just fabric.

But when it's worn with intention, it becomes a mission. It becomes a memory. It becomes the truth.

My advice to women is simple. Don't stay stuck in "this is how I grew up." Be open, ask and learn. Try and adjust. Life isn't meant to be comfortable, it's meant to be meaningful.

mitzvah can gently open a door for another.

Meirav Aftalion is the founder of Queen Esther Mitpachot, a *Torah*-inspired head-covering brand born from personal struggle and purpose. An Israeli mom of four based in LA, she shares *mitpachot, tzniut,* and real-life *Torah* on Instagram—empowering women to embrace dignity, faith, and individuality.

🌐 **Queenesthermitpachot.com**

RUNNING FROM PHARAOH:
Freeing the Ego Within

BY: ZLATA EHRENSTEIN

"SPLITTING THE SEA" BY PENINA SCHLEIDER

Let us take a closer look at *Pharaoh*, the tyrant who ruled *Mitzrayim*, and how he was dismantled and completely crushed as the *Yidden*, after 210 years, took their belongings and great wealth, journeyed toward the Red Sea, crossed it, and advanced toward *Har Sinai* to receive the *Torah*.

The *Zohar* explains that the word *Pharaoh* shares the same letters as **הָעוֹרֶף** (*ha'oref*), the shoulder bone. When *Pharaoh* exudes power, believing that no one and nothing can stand in his way, it is reflected in our posture and body language.

Take a closer look at your own body language. The very moments when I feel entitled, when no one dares tell me otherwise, are the moments when my *Pharaoh* is enraged and taking control of my life. We justify it by saying, "It's coming to me," "I can't tolerate any other behavior," or "This is my house, and I decide."

This can sound very legitimate. However, when the motive is not aligned with *Torah* values, we are allowing our inner *Pharaoh* to claim authority over us.

TIP #1 What makes me obnoxious or intolerant? When do my neck muscles tense and make me jerk?

Hashem told *Moshe Rabbeinu* exactly how to dissolve this false belief. The secret hidden in the Ten Plagues is our guide. Once we identify who our *Pharaoh* is, we can rid ourselves of these aspects of life, with the plagues and their messages revealing the code for healthy, balanced relationships.

BLOOD – The Nile River was the idol of the Egyptians. It overflowed once a year, irrigating all the fields. No rain fell in *Mitzrayim*; no one ever looked upward toward the heavens or *Hashem* to ask for sustenance. Everything was nature-oriented. These false beliefs are the first to rid ourselves of. We must change belief in nature to passion for *Hashem*. Blood represents heat and

excitement in our lives. Water is inanimate, the lowest level of the four elements of creation, with the least visible life or holiness. Recognize that these areas, too, are constantly directed by *Hashem*.

TIP #2 Check yourself: where is my belief system? How much is Torah-oriented, and how much is nature-inclined?

FROGS – Frogs live in water. Water is cold, pointing to areas in life where we are apathetic or emotionally distant. The frogs were even willing to jump into hot ovens, changing their innate nature to fulfill the command of *Hashem*. The second step in leaving *Mitzrayim* is training ourselves to go against our basic nature and become passionate about fulfilling *Hashem's* will.

The frogs arrived at a time when there was a dispute over the exact border of *Mitzrayim* and its neighbor, Libya. The frogs only invaded Egyptian land, not the neighboring territory. From this, we learn that borders are

inherent to creation. *Hashem* established boundaries and healthy structure for life. When we tamper with these borders in any area of life, we invite chaos.

TIP #3 a) When and where do I go beyond myself, willing to forego personal comfort? Are my boundaries man-made or Torah-directed?
b) In which areas, and to what extent, am I willing to go against my nature to do the will of Hashem?

LICE – This tiny creeping insect was too small for the Egyptian magicians to replicate. Here, they were forced to admit that this was something only *Hashem* could create. Once we negate the idol of nature, we infuse life with true belief in *Hashem*, to the extent that even the smallest details of daily life are directed through *hashgacha pratit*. There are no exceptions.

TIP #4 How do I react to the little things in my life? Do I truly believe they, too, are directed by Hashem?

WILD ANIMALS – Here, a mixture of wild animals invaded the entire country and attacked only the Egyptians. They bit, frightened, and killed. There is no explanation for how they distinguished between Egyptians and Jews other than the fact that *Hashem* directed them to each individual. The Egyptians were forced to admit that *Hashem* is in control.

TIP #5 Do I truly trust that Hashem will save me? Or do I believe that disasters, animals, rebels, or terrorists control life?

DEATH OF LIVESTOCK – A deadly virus spread among the animals, killing all that remained. Even animals housed in Jewish homes were struck.

TIP #6 How do I relate to anything harmful or interfering with my income, health, or parnassah? Do I truly believe that Hashem orchestrates even the areas where I invest so much effort?

BOILS – The plagues were systematic. They began with what was farthest from personal life, the Nile River. Gradually, they moved closer: the fields, the animals, and finally the body itself.

TIP #7 Is there a difference in how I react to tragedies happening far away versus those close to home?

HAIL – A miraculous mixture of fire encased in ice fell from the sky. Fire should have melted the ice, or the ice should have extinguished the fire. Neither happened. Instead, they burned with ice and fire simultaneously. Only the Egyptians suffered. The message is that *Hashem* can sustain opposing forces at the same time. Nothing is beyond His power. He is infinite and beyond the limits of nature and human logic.

TIP #8 How comfortable am I accepting events beyond my control? Can I live with a Supernatural Power beyond nature and human reasoning?

LOCUSTS – At this point, the power of *Hashem* was undeniable. We are the chosen people, and none of the *Yidden* suffered.

TIP #9 Can I develop healthy self-esteem and feel proud to be chosen to serve the King of the Universe?

DARKNESS – The *Yidden* were already purified and eager to leave *Mitzrayim*. During this plague, they entered Egyptian homes to identify where valuables were kept. Jewelry symbolizes the spiritual and physical wealth promised to *Avraham Avinu*. Neighbors represent the areas of life we encounter only occasionally.

TIP #10 Can I take an honest inventory of my possessions, noting what I truly need in my service of Hashem? Are there items I can leave behind?

DEATH OF THE FIRSTBORN – *Hashem* strikes at what is most precious: life itself. This is when *Pharaoh* finally panics and begs the *Yidden* to leave.

TIP #11 When my Pharaoh panics, how do I respond? Do I apologize, or do I try to dominate completely?

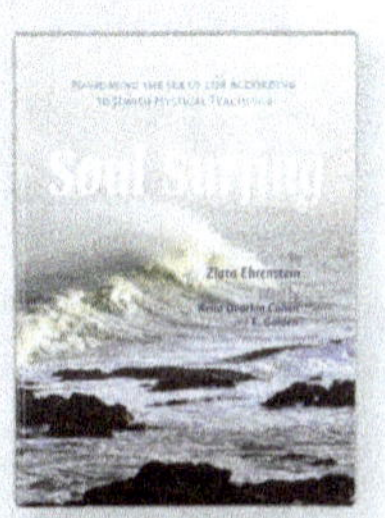

Zlata Ehrenstein was born and raised in Brooklyn and currently lives in *Tzfas*. Her passion is *tefila*, *Tehillim*, and studying *Torah* as a personal guide to daily life. Classes are offered in person and on Zoom, along with weekly short tips.

- zlatae@gmail.com
- soulsurfing.org

A Pesach Journal for Leaving Mitzrayim

BY: NECHAMA DINA WASSERMAN-LABER

Pesach is a time to challenge limiting beliefs and free ourselves from spiritual boundaries.

The *Haggadah* lays out the order, using stories, rituals, and questions to guide us step by step from personal limitation to freedom.

Journaling has always been my quiet refuge.

After losing my father as a child of 10, my journal held what I couldn't yet say out loud, giving grief, questions, and hope a safe place to land.

This article includes guided journaling prompts inspired by the *Haggadah*, inviting you to answer in your journal transforming reflection into personal redemption.

Step 1: Thank G-d in Advance

Trust and courage open the door to redemption. The Jews were commanded to celebrate the *Seder*, sacrifice a lamb, and eat *matzah* and bitter herbs while still in Egypt. They earned redemption by trusting G-d and acting courageously, even when it seemed impossible.

♥ **JOURNAL:** How can you strengthen your trust in G-d and act with courage to leave your personal Egypt? Thank *Hashem* in advance for redeeming you from your personal Egypt.

Step 2: Show Readiness

The Jews were instructed to eat the *Pesach* offering "with your waist belted, your shoes on your feet, and your staff in your hand" (*Shemos* 12:11). They had to be fully prepared for redemption even while still in bondage, showing readiness, courage, and trust in freedom.

Preparation for redemption requires growth within yourself, your environment, and the wider world.

Belt – Refine Yourself: Choose upright conduct and perform *mitzvos*.

♥ **JOURNAL:** How can you improve your character and bring joy to a *mitzvah*?

Shoes – Help Others: Step outside yourself to enhance the lives of others.

♥ **JOURNAL:** Who in your immediate environment needs your help?

Staff – Impact the World: Reach further with your gifts.

♥ **JOURNAL:** What tools and talents can you use to impact the wider world?

(Adapted from a letter by the Lubavitcher Rebbe)

Step 3: Use the Strengths Inherited from Our Mothers

The Matriarchs provide four keys to redemption. The four cups of wine at the *Seder* symbolize the 4 Matriarchs. (Rabbi Yeshayal Halevi Horowitz).

SARAH – Trust in *Hashem*

The 1st Cup of *Kiddush* thanks *Hashem* for separating us from the nations. *Sarah Imeinu* teaches us to strengthen faith and inspire others to trust in One G-d.

RIVKA – Overcome the Past

The 2nd Cup used during the story of the Exodus reminds us that we can rise above our past. *Rivka Imeinu* chose kindness and truth despite her upbringing.

ROCHEL – Recognize Goodness

The 3rd Cup, with the Grace After Meals recognizes how G-d sustains us and sends helpers, as *Rochel's* son *Yosef* sustained the family during famine.

TAMBOURINE: BY CHANA RACHEL GAFFIN

LEAH – Express Gratitude

The 4th Cup during *Hallel* thanks G-d, as *Leah Imeinu* lived with gratitude.

♥ **JOURNAL:** How can you use the strengths of our Mothers to bring redemption?

Step 4: Ma Nishtana – Ask Questions

The Four Questions are asked even when no child is physically present because we are *Hashem*'s child. We answer the inner child with words of truth and trust.

1. Night = Challenge

QUESTION: What makes this challenge different? Why is it important?

2. Salt Water = Tears

On all nights we don't dip, but on this night we dip twice.

QUESTION: How can you dip into tears to pray sincerely, heal, and grow?

3. *Matzah* = Humility

On all nights we eat leavened bread or *matzah*, and on this night only *matzah* (which is not puffed).

QUESTION: How can you release ego and embrace humility to leave your Egypt?

4. Bitter Herbs = Pain

On all nights we eat various vegetables, and on this night, bitter herbs.

QUESTION: How can you seek support and sweeten the pain in times of bitterness?

♥ **JOURNAL:** Find a childhood photo and write your inner child a letter offering hope, trust and reassurance of *Hashem*'s unconditional love.

Step 5: Pray & G.R.O.W.

Prayer is a path to freedom. It liberates the soul from limitation and helps us return to ourselves and to *Hashem*. The order of prayer in the *Siddur* offers a gentle structure for this journey, guiding us from awareness to connection and then to asking.

If it helps, try holding one part of prayer at a time. Not as a method to memorize, just as four simple directions for your heart.

G – GRATITUDE: Morning blessings (*Birchat HaShachar*)

♥ **JOURNAL:** List three blessings you are grateful for.

R – RECOGNITION: Verses of praise (*Baruch She'amar–Yishtabach*)

♥ JOURNAL: Where do you notice *Hashem*'s kindness or wonders in your day?

O – ONENESS: The *Shema* and its blessings

♥ JOURNAL: How can you reveal faith in *Hashem* through your thoughts, speech, and actions?

W – WANTS / WISHES: The *Amidah* (*Shemoneh Esrei*)

♥ JOURNAL: What is one wish you want to bring to *Hashem* to help you fulfill your mission?

May we merit the light of the Ultimate Redemption and be blessed to spend this *Pesach* together in Jerusalem!

Nechama Dina Wasserman-Laber is a mother of 11 and grandmother, an educator, retreat director, "GROW" life coach, and author, including My *Haggadah* Journal and the GROW Method of Prayer. She is the founder of JGU Press, JGR Leadership Campus, and global communities for girls at:
🌐 **JewishGirlsUnite.com**
and for women at
🌐 **GROWConnectionNetwork.com.**

SPONSORED

בס"ד

Mirrors and Apples –
REFLECTIONS OF WOMEN ON THE SEDER PLATE

BY: RABBANIT SHANI TARAGIN

SINKS AND "SELFIES"

Sefer Shemot opens paradoxically with the anonymity of heroes. The book of names begins with nameless women: midwives, mothers, sisters, and daughters, whose shared traits of seeing (r.a.h), fearing (y.r.a), and saving, sustain life amidst darkness. As *Chazal* teach, just as Shifrah and Puah defied Pharaoh's decree to murder the newborns, countless righteous women sowed the seeds of redemption through moral courage, faith, and love.

The righteousness of women continued in the wilderness where they displayed consistent faith and devotion. They resisted their husband's requests of golden jewelry for the idolatrous calf, and led the men in coming to the *Mishkan* with their contributions. Rashi (*Shemot* 38:8), quoting *Midrash Tanchuma* (*Pekudei* 9), recounts that the women's mirrors used to fashion the wash basin were explicitly mentioned among the copper donations to highlight the women's role in redemption. *Moshe* initially wished to reject them until *Hashem* declared: "Accept them; these are dearer to Me than all other contributions, for through them the women raised the hosts of Israel in Egypt. For when their husbands were tired through the crushing labor they used to bring them food and drink and encouraged them to eat. Then **they would take the mirrors, and each gazed at herself in her mirror together with her husband,** saying endearingly to him, "*See, I am more beautiful than you!*" Thus they awakened their husbands' affection and subsequently became the mothers of many children, as it is said, *"Under the apple tree I awakened you"* (*Shir HaShirim* 8:5).

These mirrors were, in essence, the first "selfies"—not instruments of vanity, but reflections of love,

memory, and faith. The women used them to mirror not despair, but determination—to remind their husbands and themselves of a shared beauty of past and present, and destiny that transcended servitude. Through this act of reflection, they ensured the future of *Am Yisrael.*

The *Shelah HaKadosh* (Rabbi Yeshayahu HaLevi Horowitz) teaches that women are the consistent catalysts of redemption precisely because they understand the nature of light and reflection. Like the moon, they do not generate light but receive, refract, and redirect it, transforming darkness into illumination. Their mirrors, symbols of reflective consciousness, were brought under the apple trees, where remembrance of beauty of the past inspired love, and new life blossomed amid affliction to create a glorious future. Women perceive not only the image before them but the continuum of past, present, and future, embodying the redemptive power of hope and memory intertwined.

THE APPLE ON THE SEDER PLATE

"In the merit of the righteous women of that generation, Israel was redeemed from Egypt" (Sotah 11b).

This assertion is richly elaborated by Rabbi Avira (*Shemot Rabbah 1,12*) who reveals the apple tree as a central symbol of redemption. He teaches that when the women of Israel went out to draw water, *Hashem* miraculously provided them with small

fish in their jars which they would bring as nourishment to their exhausted husbands in the fields. The women would prepare food and drink, bathing and anointing their husbands, and restoring to them dignity and vitality. Within the confines of oppression, the women created protected spaces of intimacy and reassurance—moments of closeness that rekindled hope and desire as they were determined to raise the next generation despite Pharaoh's decrees. When the women conceived, they returned home. When the time came to give birth, **they went out to the fields and delivered their children beneath the apple trees,** concealed from Egyptian eyes yet sustained by hope in the future, as it is written: *"Under the apple tree I awakened you"* (*Shir HaShirim* 8:5).

This *Midrash* reframes redemption as emerging not only from suffering, but from faith-filled creativity, intimacy, and continuity. The apple tree thus becomes a locus of courage and renewal—where memory of love gives rise to a fertile future of nationhood.

Against this backdrop, the symbolism of *charoset* becomes especially resonant. The *Mishnah* (*Pesachim* 10:3) debates whether eating *charoset* on *Seder* night is a *mitzvah*. The *Gemara* (*Pesachim* 116b) records two explanations for Rabbi Eliezer ben Tzadok's ruling that it is indeed obligatory:

Rabbi Levi explains that *charoset* commemorates the apple tree, while Rabbi Yochanan teaches that it recalls the clay and mortar of enslavement. Abaye concludes that *charoset* must therefore be both tart and thick—tart to evoke the apple, thick to recall the clay (*Rashi*, ibid.)

These two interpretations represent complementary lenses of collective memory. Rabbi Yochanan emphasizes the men's backbreaking labor in the clay of oppression; Rabbi Levi highlights the women's courage beneath the apple tree, where hope and life were quietly restored. *Charoset* thus embodies a dialectic of pain and promise as essential components in retelling the story of *Yetziat Mitzrayim*. When prepared with apples, it recalls sweetness, intimacy, and renewal; when dense, it evokes the weight of servitude.

On *Seder* night, the apple on the plate invites us to remember that redemption was born not only from *Hashem*'s response to suffering in the present, but from the women who nurtured life, continuity, and faith in the future.

REFLECTIONS OF REDEMPTION

Seder night invites us to look into the mirrors of our history—to see in our collective reflection both the bitterness and the sweetness, the clay and the apple. As we dip our *maror* into *charoset*, we reenact this union of pain and promise, despair and determination.

The righteous women of Egypt teach us that redemption begins with reflection— with the courage to see beauty amid brokenness and to transform memory into movement. Their mirrors and apples remind us that faith in the future is born from those who can look backward with memory of love and forward with eternal hope—a message as vital *ba'yamim ha'hem* as it is *bazman hazeh*.

Rabbanit Shani Taragin is an educator and educational director at Matan, leading major *Tanach* and *Torah Shebe'al Peh* teacher-training programs. She teaches, leads *Tanach* tours, and lectures worldwide on *Tanach*, Jewish education, *halacha*, and women's health. Shani lives with her family in Alon Shvut, Gush Etzion.

Waiting at the Shore

BY: SHIRA LANKIN SHEPS

On the *Seder* night after we were attacked by Iran for the first time, I was already in tears before we reached the opening songs.

Only days had passed since we watched missiles fly toward us on live television, since we sat through long hours of dread, and ran with pounding hearts into our bomb shelter, unsure what the world would look like if we emerged again.

I remember stepping out afterward in awe. I carried the awareness that we had just experienced a revealed miracle. Our country woke the next dawn unscathed, and we, its citizens, were bleary-eyed, shaken, and grateful for the Divine intervention we had witnessed.

So when it came time to sit down at the *Seder*, the night came alive to me in a whole new way.

We moved through the familiar choreography, but for the first time, the Seder did not feel like a reenactment. It felt like a language we had been given for moments exactly like this.

We spoke about our present: my brothers in *miluim*, the sacrifices so many families were carrying, the relentless threats that shadowed our daily lives.

Maror: In the Wild Plants of Israel

SHULIE WISMAN

The Torah tells us that *"merorim"* are the side dish for your Passover sacrifice, along with the obligatory matzah:

וְאָכְלוּ אֶת הַבָּשָׂר בַּלַּיְלָה הַזֶּה צְלִי אֵשׁ וּמַצּוֹת עַל מְרֹרִים יֹאכְלֻהוּ נִשְׁמַת יְבֻשׁ

"They shall eat the flesh that same night; they shall eat it roasted over the fire, with unleavened bread and with bitter herbs" (Exodus 12:8).

Rashi takes note of the plural form and adds: "All bitter plants are called 'maror.'"

This seems to leave the options wide open, as long as we define what a plant is and what bitter means.

The mishnah however, gives a very specific list:

וְאֵלּוּ יְרָקוֹת שֶׁאָדָם יוֹצֵא בָּהֶן יְדֵי חוֹבָתוֹ בְּפֶסַח, בַּחֲזֶרֶת וּבְעֻלְשִׁין וּבְתַמְכָא וּבְחַרְחֲבִינָה וּבְמָרוֹר. (משנה פסחים ב:ו)

"And these are the herbs with which one discharges his obligation on Pesach: with lettuce [hazaret]; with chicory [olshin]; with wild chicory [tamkah]; with picridium [harhavina], and with sonchus [maror]. (Mishnah Pesahim 2:6)

Can we identify these plants? Although there are many controversies, some plants are easier to label than others. Everyone agrees that *"hazaret"* is lettuce, specifically romaine lettuce. The Gemara has a lovely pun about lettuce and why we use it for maror. Lettuce in Hebrew is חסה (hasah), because God had mercy (חס) on us and took us out of Egypt.

Olesh/עולש is translated by the Gemara as *"hindevi"*—we know that as endive. Endive and chicory are related to each other, their young leaves are soft and later become hard. Maimonides thinks that *tamcha/תמכא*, one of the more mysterious of the plants, is also a type of endive. *Harhavina/חרחבינה* is another tricky one. Yehuda Felix, eminent scholar of material life in the Bible, as well as Bar-Ilan University professor Zohar Amar, following Maimonides, define it as a plant called *Eryngium creticum*. This plant was known by the Arabs as Abraham's thorn or the Jews' thorn, showing that they knew Jews used it for Pesach. Like many of the others listed here, the Eryngium starts out with soft young leaves. However, by the summer, these leaves are dead and new thorny leaves grow. This transformation is what the rabbis are referring to when they see the allegorical side to maror:

"Rabbi Samuel bar Nahmani said that Rabbi Yohanan said: Why are the Egyptians likened to bitter herbs to tell you that just as these bitter herbs are soft at first and harsh in the end, so too, the Egyptians were soft at first, but were harsh in the end." (Pesahim 39)

Finally, the mishnah lists maror, or as the Gemara calls it, *merirata*. This is a weed called the sowthistle, which has yellow flowers in the summer. This is the favored maror of the Samaritans, who eat it alongside the Passover sacrifice that they prepare every year on Mount Gerizim.

All these types of maror are wild plants of the land of Israel, familiar to those who lived here. As time passed and Jews lived further away from the land, they lost this knowledge. In addition, Pesach falls in the early spring and the greens listed here may not have been ripe yet in the cold climate of Europe. By the 17th century, Rabbi Yom Tov Lipman Heller of Prague defined the *tamcha* of the mishnah as *chrein*, horseradish root, and it became popular on the seder plates of Eastern European Jews, despite it clearly not being a plant that grew in the land of Israel in the time of the Mishnah.

So romaine or *chrein*? Now that we are fortunate to have returned to the land of Israel and to have begun learning its botanical secrets, eat your *maror* from the fruits of the land, which are sweet even when they are bitter. •

> *Eat your maror from the fruits of the land, which are sweet even when they are bitter.*

The establishment of the State of Israel has made it possible to return to many "original" aspects of the Torah and the Mishnah. How is your experience of Judaism affected by the existence of the State of Israel?

We spoke about the hostages and what it means to have your freedom stolen. About the swell of antisemitism rising across the world, and the loneliness of feeling misunderstood in the places we once expected safety.

It was one of the most meaningful *Sederim* I can remember. Because the truth is that once you have lived inside history, once you have felt fear in your body and not only in your imagination, the Seder changes. The *Haggadah* stops being a book about the past and becomes a vessel for the present: a ritual designed to hold panic and praise in the same breath. To make room for grief alongside faith and gratitude. To name bitterness, and still keep walking toward redemption.

Over these last two years, I worked with Rachel Sharansky Danziger and Rabbanit Anne Gordon to co-edit and publish a series called *Az Nashir*. We Will Sing Again. We wrote and workshopped *tehinot*, prayers in our own mother tongues, as Jewish women have done for generations, responding to the spiritual demands of daily life. We wrote about life during the war, and the new world and reality we were experiencing.

As time moved on, I realized that *Pesach* demanded its own language.

So my publishing imprint, The SHVILLI Center and The Layers Press, partnered with Matan Women's Institute for *Torah* Studies to create a *Haggadah* that feels urgently necessary for this time. With seventy-two contributors who are teachers, scholars, artists, therapists, and writers, we wove modern commentaries, essays, and prayers directly into the *Haggadah* text, alongside visual art and photography, not as decoration, but as another form of *midrash*.

I am humbled by the process of working with my teachers from Matan, and with friends and colleagues, to create something so ambitious. More than

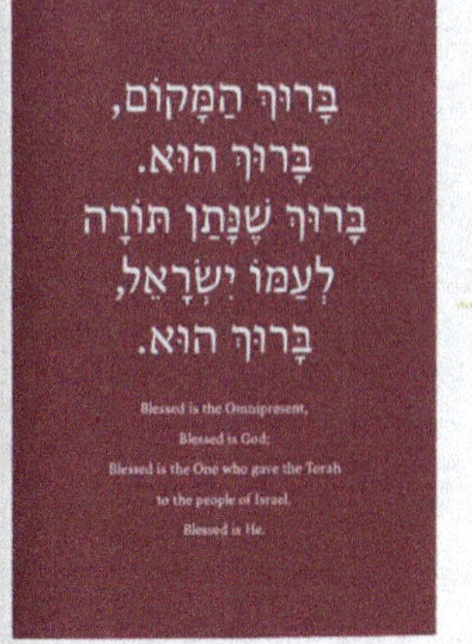

that, I believe it reflects what Jewish women in Israel are carrying right now: a fierce determination to build language, meaning, and spiritual resilience while we are still inside the fire.

We need more *Torat HaNefesh*, *Torah* of the soul, in our generation. Today, women are learning *Torah* in unprecedented depth, developing the tools not only to interpret our sacred texts, but to bring them into conversation with real life. That isn't only an achievement; it is an opportunity.

Chazal teach that the generation that left Egypt merited redemption through the righteous women who believed it would come, and helped bring it into reality. And they teach that the final redemption will mirror the first: that those who hold on to faith, even in darkness, help bring the light closer.

So I ask: what does it mean to live as women of faith in a time like this? What does it mean to believe in *geulah* while the world feels fractured, while our people grieve, while our soldiers fight, while we brace for what we cannot predict?

This *Pesach*, as we move through our traditional text, we do not have to keep our present outside the door.

The *Haggadah* insists that we experience the story personally, as if we ourselves are leaving Egypt now. It makes room for new stories to enter its living corpus. It gives us words for the moments when we are raw, and a melody for the moments when we are overwhelmed.

So fill your table with chapters of the now. Let your children hear you speak honestly about fear and faith. Taste the bitterness when you name what has been lost, those who never came home, and those still waiting to. And then remember that in every generation they rise against us, and in every generation we survive.

Sing out the miracles you have witnessed. Thank God for the gifts of protection, family, courage, and endurance. And if your voice shakes when you sing, sing anyway.

Because the *Seder* has only ever asked us to keep retelling and reliving the story.

It asks us to wait at the shore, believing that the sea can split once again.

Shira Lankin Sheps, MSW is the Executive Director of The SHVILLI Center, founder and publisher of The Layers Project & Press, and author of Layers: Stories of Struggle, Resilience, and Growth from Jewish Women. She is also co-editor of the *Az Nashir* series, writer and workshop facilitator, and spends her time amplifying women's voices in *Torah*, prayer, and contemporary Jewish life.

 **shvillicenter.org**

Shiralsheps@shvillicenter.org

Around the Pesach Table:
Minhagim That Make a Home

BY: SHOSHANNA STEIN BENARROCH

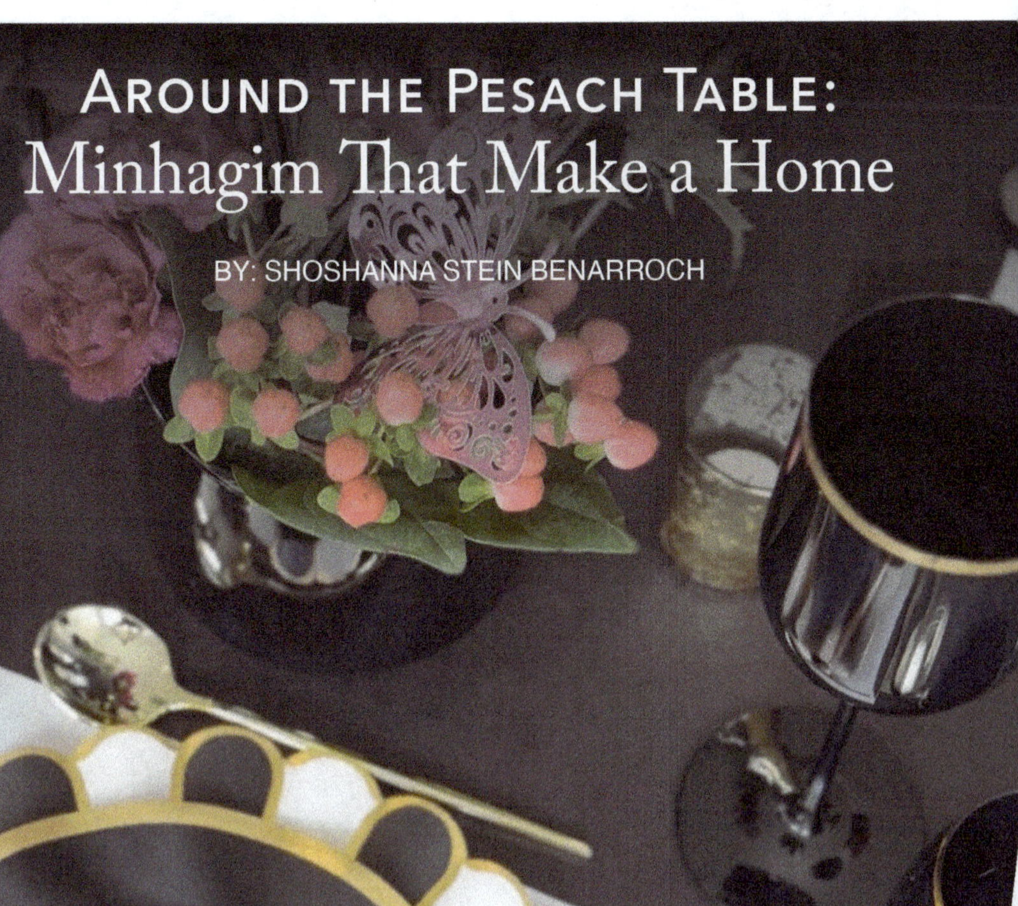

Minhagim are the small things that make a Jewish home feel like home. They are the sounds, tastes, and moments that return every *Pesach* and quietly remind us where we belong. Some are handed down through generations. Others are created along the way, shaped by the families we build.

In this feature, five women share one *Pesach minhag* that lives in their home. Nothing polished or prescriptive. Just real moments, real memories, and the traditions that make their *Pesach* table feel personal, meaningful, and alive.

meaningful, a moment that connects generations and invites everyone in.

What matters most to me is that everyone feels seen. Everyone has a chair, space in front of them, and room for their *minhagim* to be honored. Our table becomes a place of belonging, where tradition is not diluted by blending, but strengthened by it.

Here are some beautiful and inspiring *minhagim* shared by women from all over the world.

SHOSHANNA STEIN BENARROCH

Contemporary Judaic artist, creative educator, founder of the Ki Tov Project, and social media creator rooted in community and Jewish life. @MySoCalledJewishLife

One of the *minhagim* that feels most alive in our home is not a single custom, but the intentional blending of *minhagim*. Our family brings together Ashkenazi and Sephardi roots, and over time I have learned that honoring tradition does not mean choosing one story over another. It means making space at the table for everyone.

Our *Yom Tov* table reflects that blend. The food is a mix of Ashkenazi and Sephardi dishes and *simanim*. The songs move between different *nusachot*, some familiar, some newly learned, all part of one shared experience.

At our *Pesach Seder*, this comes to life most clearly. We begin with the Sephardi *bibelu* ceremony, singing while the *Seder* plate is gently tapped on each person's head. It is joyful, playful, and deeply

CHANALE FELLIG

Writer, singer, and storyteller based in Israel @mybeautifullandofisrael

Pesach at my Chabad grandparents' house had rules that were not up for discussion. No processed food. No *gebrochts*. No *kitniyot*. The adults took this very seriously. My Bubby boiled sugar on the stove, cooked with chicken schmaltz, and peeled every single vegetable by hand and somehow everything came out perfect anyway.

The children, however, were given one quiet exception, and it felt like winning the lottery.

We were allowed dairy and chocolate.

While the grown ups hovered over pots and checked labels for the tenth time, we sat at the kitchen table with bowls of cottage cheese and sour cream, completely unconcerned. Then came the chocolate syrup. Thick, glossy, poured without restraint. My Bubby would add her candies and nuts, sliding them across the table like contraband, her eyes sparkling.

To this day, sour cream mixed with chocolate syrup does not taste like a strange combination to me. It tastes like *Pesach*. It tastes like freedom, indulgence, and being loved.

My Bubby is 95 now. She is alive, sharp, and still eating her cottage cheese. Every *Pesach*, that taste brings me right back to her kitchen, and I know exactly why it still matters.

SHOSHANA BILLYACK

Massage therapist, reflexologist, and doula based in RBS Alef, supporting women's wellness through every stage of life.

A Passover Culinary Adventure: Our Family's Spirited *Minhag*

Passover is a joyous celebration of freedom and our heritage! Our family has a delightful *minhag* that brings a unique burst of fun to the *Seder*. As we transition to the *Shulchan Orech* meal, we kick things off with a lively ritual! Beyond the symbolic egg in salt water, celebrating renewal, we add a playful twist by crushing *matzah* directly into it. This joyful way of honoring "*gebrochts*" makes the start of the meal an extra special, memorable moment for our whole family.

We savored each bite, realizing that sometimes the most unusual traditions are the ones we love the most!

Aleeza Ben Shalom

Relationship coach, matchmaker, Netflix's Jewish Matchmaking, host of The Jewish Matchmaker podcast, and founder of the Jewish Matchmaking Movement. @AleezaBenShalom

As Passover approached, my husband and I prepared for our first *Seder* together. Growing up, my family had an unusual tradition: we would take gefilte fish from a jar and plate it, then boil the jelly, and soak *matzah* in it, adding just the right amount of salt and pepper. It was our little ritual, and we called it *Matzah* in fish "uch." We only said it and never spelled it so I don't even know if that's how it's spelled.

When the family gathered for dinner, they exchanged stories, and suddenly, laughter erupted. "You do that too?" they asked, looking at us in disbelief. It turned out they had shared the same tradition in their own homes, though we had never known anyone else who practiced it.

This simple dish, once just ours, became a bridge between our families.

Anat Ishai (Challah Mom)

Jewish lifestyle digital creator sharing her Jewish journey through *challah*, dance, Israel, and Jewish wisdom. @ChallahMom

My most memorable Passover tradition was singing *Ma Nishtana*. As the designated youngest child in my nuclear family this was a special moment for me to have the stage. I used to practice my lines and clear my throat and belt it proudly for my family. While we never had a long traditional *Seder*, my family opted for the express version. *Seder* night was always with my parents, grandparents and my brother, until I got married and we had our four children. As each child had their opportunity to sing the four questions, I always had vivid memories of doing the same in my grandparents dining room. Now I proudly hand the tradition to my youngest child and create new memories and traditions in our home in Israel.

Jezliah: The Freedom to Sing and Dance

BY: ANNIE ORENSTEIN

Each and every one of us has a unique light and purpose to share. We are all on a journey to discover, develop and define this purpose and become our best selves.

I first met Jezliah in 2018 after a show I produced near Beit Shemesh. The next day she told me something that stayed with me. After her conversion to Judaism, she had stepped away from performing. For a time, the stage went quiet.

But some gifts are not meant to stay hidden.

Something inside her began to awaken again. Not ego. Not ambition. Calling.

And when she returned to music, it wasn't the same kind of performance. It was deeper. Rooted. Aligned. Her voice became not just expression, but connection.

I understood that her musical mission was something deep.

A fire that was rekindled inside her and a vision to uplift women and girls became her goal in life.

Her voice wasn't only technically strong. It carried history. Choice. Courage.

Today, her music inspires hundreds of women and girls. But what moves me most is not the applause. It is the integrity. The journey.

The decision to use her talent in a way that reflects who she has become.

As we approach *Pesach*, the season of freedom, Jezliah's story reminds us that freedom is not only about leaving Egypt.

Sometimes it is about reclaiming the part of yourself that was always meant to sing.

Jezliah, let us start with your journey. How did you find your voice as a Jewish singer, songwriter, producer, and dance academy co-founder?

My journey truly begins with my conversion to Judaism. Choosing this path reshaped the direction of my entire life. Looking back now, I can see how *Hashem* was quietly aligning every step long before I understood where I was headed. What once felt like separate chapters, music, dance, teaching, and faith, were all preparation for the path I was meant to walk.

Finding my voice was not a straight line. For many years I was helping others grow, express themselves, and shine. While that work was meaningful, there was a deeper voice inside me that had not fully emerged yet. I was carrying something more personal and more vulnerable that needed space to exist.

Throughout my life and journey, I experienced loss, pain, and many challenges. Through it all, my relationship with *Hashem* was always on the front line. It was during those moments of struggle that the music began to flow out of me. The songs were personal, raw, and deeply honest.

I did not know if I had the courage to release something so vulnerable into the

Jewish world. But when I finally did, the response surprised me. Women and girls connected to the words and emotions they themselves were carrying.

That is when I understood that this music was filling a real need. By allowing myself to be fully seen, I created space for others to feel seen too. My voice stopped trying to fit into what already existed and instead began creating what was missing. That is when my work became more than music. It became a mission, unfolding exactly the way *Hashem* planned.

You have been described as a role model for young women. How do you weave freedom and modesty into your music and dance?

I see freedom and modesty as partners, not opposites. True freedom comes from living in alignment with my values. When I am grounded in who I am, I am more expressive, not less. Modesty gives my creativity intention and depth.

Empowerment comes from choice. I choose how I show up and how I express emotion. Dance does not need to be provocative to be powerful, and music does not need to cross boundaries to be deeply felt.

There is strength in self respect, beauty in restraint, and confidence in knowing your worth. When freedom is rooted in purpose, it becomes something that elevates you.

When you are on stage, what does freedom feel like to you?

Freedom on stage happens when my voice, heart, and body become vessels for something bigger than myself. I am not performing for approval. I am singing and moving in conversation with *Hashem*. Music and dance become *tefillah*.

Sharing that *tefillah* with my Jewish sisters makes it even more powerful. I want girls to see that music can be sacred, expressive, and powerful, and that they can embrace their own voices within the Jewish world.

I remember one performance where I debuted a very special song and danced alongside my best friend. What began as a performance became a moment of healing and new beginnings. The intention was to connect us in love and gratitude to *Hashem*. It was deeply transformative for everyone in the room.

This is what freedom feels like on stage. A release, a surrender, and a connection beyond words.

Can you share about your creative process and how you balance family, marriage, and career?

My creative process starts with prayer and honesty. I let music and movement flow naturally from real moments and experiences. The most powerful art comes from vulnerability and connection.

Balancing family, marriage, and career requires intentionality and *bitachon*. I make space for my loved ones just as I make space for my music. There is no separation between creativity and life. They feed each other.

What challenges have you faced as a performer?

One of the biggest challenges has been navigating expectations within the Orthodox Jewish world while creating something new and personal. My sound is more contemporary and non-traditional. As a convert, I sometimes worried how that would be received.

I love singing traditional Jewish songs, but I am also drawn to modern expression. These questions pushed me to clarify who I am and trust my authenticity.

What advice would you offer women who feel unsure about expressing themselves?

Look deep within yourself and focus on the purpose *Hashem* has given you. Each of us has a unique mission. When you stay true to that calling rather than trying to meet others' expectations, you discover your freedom.

When your expression is aligned with your mission, it naturally inspires others. True impact comes from courage, *emunah*, and honoring the voice *Hashem* placed within you.

You do not have to shrink yourself or wait for permission to shine. Each of us has a voice, a story, and a light that is completely unique. When you create from honesty, courage, and *emunah*, it resonates far beyond what you expect.

Trust your journey. Honor your voice. Step forward bravely.

Jezliah is a Jewish singer, performer, and creative director whose music fuses *emunah*, emotional honesty, and contemporary sound. Co-founder of RBS Dance and Music Academy, she creates meaningful experiences that uplift women and girls, telling stories of faith, growth, and connection to *Hashem* through song and stage.

Annie Orenstein has been producing shows for women and girls since 2006. In 2010, she co-founded Spotlight On Women. She is passionate about producing open mics for performers to grow professionally and for Jewish women to be inspired. She also hosted Spotlight On Women Radio, and writes in local newspapers and magazines highlighting artists. She lives in Maaleh Adumim with her family.
Annie.spotlight@gmail.com

Penina Schleider
ART OF INNER REDEMPTION

EXCLUSIVELY FOR HER TRIBE MAGAZINE

For Penina Schleider, painting has never been just a skill or a profession. From the early years of sketching for hours as a child, through her formal training in Jerusalem, art has been a space of listening, growth, and quiet connection. In this interview, she shares how creativity, faith, and life experience come together in her work, and how her understanding of Geulah, Pesach, and personal renewal has been shaped not only on the canvas, but through the journey of living itself.

CAN YOU TELL US ABOUT THE HEART BEHIND YOUR GEULAH PIECE ON THE BACK COVER AND WHAT GEULAH MEANS TO YOU?

I have carried the idea of *Geulah* with me for many years. As a nation, we long for the *Beit HaMikdash*, for unity, and for *Hashem's* light to be revealed. At its heart, *Geulah* is about leaving *galut* and coming home.

The painting depicts people moving forward together toward the light, symbolizing our shared dream and the *Geulah* we can already feel. The *shofar* in the sky calls us to awaken, reflecting our connected *neshamot*.

PESACH IS A TIME OF RENEWAL AND REBIRTH. HOW ARE THESE THEMES EXPRESSED IN YOUR ARTISTIC JOURNEY, BOTH PERSONALLY AND CREATIVELY?

Pesach has always been a time of deep connection for me, to *Hashem* and to myself. I remember my father leading the *Seder* with such emotion, teaching us that *Pesach* is not just a night, but a moment of closeness with *Hashem*.

There was a period when I went through a very difficult time, for about two years I couldn't eat many foods—flour, sugar, starches. It was challenging, especially because it wasn't a "diet" I chose for a goal; it was something I had to do.

And then came *Pesach*.

I remember sitting at the *Seder*, holding the *matzah*—after asking a Rav and speaking with my doctor, knowing I needed to eat the *kezayis* I was obligated to eat. And I held it with such calm, almost like a promise. There's a phrase we say: *nahama d'mehemnusa, nahama d'asvasa*—bread of *emunah*, bread of healing. At that moment I told myself: This is not going to harm you. This can be part of your healing.

After a year of avoiding starches, eating that simple piece of *matzah* and making the *brachah*—felt like freedom. Not only physical freedom, but inner freedom: the ability to choose a new lens, trust, and life. And from that *Pesach* onward, I truly began feeling things getting better and better. I could see myself stepping out of that hard story.

WHAT IS ONE MESSAGE YOU WOULD LOVE TO LEAVE WITH WOMEN WHO ARE READY FOR THEIR OWN FRESH START THIS PESACH?

If I could leave one message for women who are ready for a fresh start this *Pesach*, it would be this: you don't need to reinvent yourself overnight. You just need to choose—one moment at a time.

Every second we're "reborn" again. We're constantly choosing. Do I speak to myself with kindness or with harshness? Do I focus on what went wrong, or do I notice what I've already overcome? Do I stay stuck in guilt—or do I forgive myself, stand up, and take the next step?

The next step doesn't have to be huge. Sometimes it's small, but real: a deep breath, quiet *tefillah*, a smile to someone when it's hard, five minutes for yourself even when you're busy, choosing to give yourself good energy instead of draining yourself with negative thoughts. Those small steps matter. They're not "small" in *Shamayim*.

So this *Pesach*, if you're ready for a fresh start, start gently. Believe in yourself. Forgive yourself. Look forward. Choose one step toward light—and trust that *Hashem* is walking with you.

WAS THERE A PERIOD IN YOUR LIFE WHEN CREATING ART BECAME A SOURCE OF HEALING OR TRANSFORMATION?

Yes, very deeply.

While pregnant with my fourth child, I discovered that this baby had completed his mission in this world and would not be coming home with us. It was heartbreaking, yet profoundly holy.

Hashem gave me strength, and the ability to see the good and feel the immense holiness in this test.

Returning to life afterward took time, emotionally and physically. Yet in that process, I received an unexpected gift: I was brought back to myself. Art, which had once felt like pressure, became a source of healing and reconnection.

This experience taught me calmness and trust, and showed me how *Hashem* carries us through every stage of life. Slowly, I chose to build my life around painting, not only as a profession, but as a calling. My work today holds more light, softness, and calm, a reminder that even in darkness, *Hashem* is present.

YOU HAVE TRAINED WITH INCREDIBLE ARTISTS. WHAT IS THE MOST PROFOUND LESSON FROM YOUR PROFESSIONAL TRAINING THAT CONTINUES TO SHAPE YOUR WORK?

Beyond technical skills, the most important lesson I learned was how we treat someone who is still learning.

As a teenager, a teacher once crossed out a drawing I was proud of. I did not fear critique, but I learned the difference between guiding growth and crushing confidence. That moment shaped how I teach and create. Art should feel safe. Growth happens best with respect and encouragement.

PESACH IS ABOUT REMOVING CHAMETZ, INCLUDING EGO AND FEAR. HOW DO YOU NAVIGATE EGO AS AN ARTIST?

Ego becomes small when you remember that we are *neshamot* from *Hashem*. I do not create myself. I use what *Hashem* gave me. Inspiration flows differently each day, and I respect that and thank *Hashem*.

When people connect to my work, I am grateful, but I remind myself that it is about the message, not about me. Gratitude and humility keep me grounded.

WHAT DOES BUILDING A SUSTAINABLE ARTISTIC CAREER LOOK LIKE TO YOU?

For me, it is a spiritual journey. Each person receives what she needs for her mission. Returning fully to art was an act of *bitachon*. My role of doing *hishtadlut* is to do the best I can using the tools *Hashem* gave me, while trusting *Hashem* with the results.

Penina Schleider is the artist behind Art by Penina, a wife and mother of six who creates light-filled, faith-inspired paintings. Her work flows from a deep connection to *Hashem*, *Torah*, and *Eretz Hakodesh*, weaving *emunah*, meaning, and calm into Jewish homes worldwide through luminous color, texture, and heartfelt commissions.

🌐 **ArtbyPenina.com**
▶ **artbypenina@gmail.com**

CHANA RACHEL GAFFIN:
PRESENCE OVER PERFECTION

A CONVERSATION
WITH
CHANA RACHEL
GAFFIN
EXCLUSIVELY FOR
HER TRIBE MAGAZINE

Feeling energized, inspired, and a little more like yourself? That's the effect Chana Rachel Gaffin tends to have on others. A fashion designer creating modest activewear for Jewish women, she connects through art, podcasting, social media, and real conversations, blending movement and creativity to uplift women in their bodies, their work, mothering and their lives, with the kind of clarity and confidence that feels like a post-workout glow.

Was there a moment in your creative or personal journey when you felt a true breakthrough, a sense that Hashem was guiding you, almost like a personal Exodus?

In 2015, just after finishing fashion school, I experienced a profound turning point. I was in the middle of becoming more religious after four years in an environment that felt disconnected from my *Yiddishkeit*. One evening, I sat by the *Chanukiah*, staring into the flames, asking *Hashem* for clarity and direction. I was waiting for a miracle, something dramatic to inspire my final collection.

Instead the breakthrough came differently. I wrote a paper on fashion and modesty and graduated.

That moment taught me something I carry with me to this day. Redemption does not always arrive in the form we expect. Sometimes it comes through surrender, through learning to let *Hashem* lead, even when the path looks different than we imagined.

When you feel blocked or disconnected, what brings you back to clarity, flow, and a sense of renewal?

Creation, in any form.

Watercolors remind me to flow. I love how the paint bleeds, moves, and creates unexpected beauty. It mirrors life so closely. When I feel blocked in fashion, I go to the fabric supplier and notice what draws me in. I close my eyes and ask myself what would make me feel beautiful in my body as it is right now.

Then I open my eyes, work with what is

in front of me, and let the process unfold. That moment of trust is often where the sea splits.

How do you balance structure with freedom in your work?

For me, it is less about *matzah* and *maror*, and more about *charoset* and *maror*.

Charoset is sweet, inviting, full of movement. That is the design process. *Maror* is the sharp discipline, finances, invoicing, meetings.

I try to front-load the *maror* at the beginning of each month so I can later give myself permission to create freely, joyfully, and from the heart.

Woman to woman, what would you say to those who struggle with self-criticism and letting go?

Your body is a gift from *Hashem*.

Self-love is not just a mindset. It is an action. When you care for your body, you build a respectful relationship with it. Do not wait for someone else to wake you up.

If you are going on a *Shabbaton* and you know you will feel better if you eat a proper breakfast, plan it. Bring it. If you know you will be happier if you exercise in the morning, pencil it in.

Make it routine. Start planting seeds. As we celebrate and learn from *Tu B'Shvat*, the fruit will come.

Is there a personal experience of releasing limiting beliefs that shaped your life?

My path to marriage took seven years. Everything shifted when I allowed myself to think differently, including dating someone younger.

I remember being engaged and attending a *Shavuot* event filled with a number of men I had once dated. I thought to myself, even if I had needed to date every single man in this room, it would not matter. When you find your soulmate, you have won. No one else matters.

Motherhood also shattered many expectations. Miscarriages, loss, and the shock of how common these experiences are. I am endlessly grateful for my children and deeply passionate about giving voice to women navigating infertility, pregnancy loss, or traumatic births.

Hearing other women's stories carried me. We should not be afraid to speak.

Can you walk us through your artistic process?

Every piece begins differently.

My latest *Chanukiah* began with transparent colored blocks I saw online, reminiscent of Aura Soma color therapy. I paired them with a mirrored base, created a mock-up, and worked with a local craftsman to carve the candle spaces. My husband and I assembled it together.

The result felt deeply intentional and full of joy.

Are there specific materials or creative practices central to your work?

For sportswear, I use an Italian lightweight fabric designed for sport and swim. I design patterns that contour the body, using color combinations that make a statement.

In art, watercolor is my language. Florals, washes, surrendering to flow. That is where I feel most myself.

When did you realize you were also a leader, not just an artist?

Thank you for the compliment!

I do not walk around thinking of myself as a leader.

I simply try to bring my gifts fully. Teaching art, designing sportswear, learning and sharing about motherhood and wellness. Wherever you are, you are a *shaliach*. That awareness shapes how you show up.

What is the most empowering lesson you have learned while building your brand?

My mother once told me, when I was still sewing everything myself,
"Chana Rachel, imagine the woman who will wear this skirt. Imagine her feeling amazing. Put that energy into the garment. She will feel it."

I try to keep that in mind when I'm creating a new collection, no matter how big!

Seeing women I don't know wearing my designs fills me with quiet pride. I've also learned to focus less on labels and more on how I want to be. Fulfillment comes from enjoying the process, not arriving at a title.

What helped you turn creativity into real sales and real impact?

Every day, do one thing for your business. One thing.

My first sale was in Tel Aviv in 2016. I had designed my first running skirt and noticed a woman running in a denim skirt. I approached her. The next morning, she was at my door placing an order.

I knew the brand was making a difference when women kept coming back, and when Beatie Deutsch won the 2019 Jerusalem Marathon wearing my skirt.

If we truly believe we are bringing Geula, what is one practical step we can take?

Carve out a set time each day to care for yourself. Exercise, meditate, do something nourishing. When you show up energized and whole, you bring your best self to the table.

How do you navigate disagreement while staying aligned?

First, I try to *ladun l'kaf zechut*, judging others favorably. I allow things to simmer before reacting.

Then I talk to *Hashem*.

Often I consult my sister, my husband, and sometimes ChatGPT.
Then I make my own decision.

Chana Rachel Gaffin (Weinberg) is a fashion designer and the creator of the modest activewear brand Chanabana. She is also an artist who teaches watercolor and motherhood-centered journaling. Raised in Beit Shemesh, she lives in Efrat with her husband and two children, drawing inspiration from movement, nature, and Jewish life.

🌐 **chanabana.com**
▶ **chana@chanabana.com**
🎙 **How She Did It**

KEEP CALM

AND COOK PESACH WITH

NAOMI NACHMAN

When it comes to *Pesach* cooking, Naomi Nachman keeps things practical, festive, and delicious. These are the kinds of recipes that earn a permanent spot on the *Yom Tov* table — smart, reliable, and made to be enjoyed.

STYLING AND PHOTOGRAPHY BY MIRIAM PASCAL COHEN

It's traditional that on the night of the *Seder* we do not eat meat that has been roasted in the oven, so I developed this stovetop meat dish for my *Pesach* catering clients to serve instead. The recipe is also ideal for *Yom Tov*, if your oven is off and you want to cook something fresh.

SEDER POT ROAST

Meat I Yields 8 servings I Freezer-friendly

Ingredients

1 tablespoon oil

1 (4-pound) California roast

2 tablespoons potato starch

1 teaspoon kosher salt

1 large onion, quartered

2 large loose carrots, cut into chunks

1 tablespoon fish-free imitation Worcestershire sauce

2 cloves garlic, minced

1 cup red wine

½ cup ketchup

¼ cup barbecue sauce

Instructions

Heat oil over high heat in a large pot or Dutch oven.

Dredge the roast on all sides in potato starch. Sear in the hot oil for a minute or less per side, until the meat starts to brown.

In a small bowl, toss together the remaining ingredients; pour over the meat. Bring to a boil, then lower to a simmer. Cover tightly and simmer for three hours, until the meat is tender.

Prepare ahead: Slice roast before freezing.

Year-round: Use flour in place of potato starch.

Cook's Note: French roast or brisket also work well in this recipe.

STYLING AND PHOTOGRAPHY BY MIRIAM PASCAL COHEN

This is one of those go-to chicken dishes you'll find yourself making again and again. Simple ingredients, bold flavor, and always a crowd-pleaser, it's perfect for a family dinner or *Yom Tov* meal.

WINNER WINNER CHICKEN DINNER

Meat | Yields 8 servings

Ingredients

2 whole chickens, cut into quarters

1 teaspoon salt

Pepper, to taste

1 cup salsa

1 cup orange jam

Zest of 1 orange (2–3 teaspoons)

1 (11-ounce) can mandarin orange pieces, drained

Instructions

Preheat the oven to 375°F.

Place chicken into a large baking pan; season with salt and pepper.

In a medium mixing bowl, stir together salsa, orange jam, zest, and mandarin oranges. Pour over chicken.

Bake, uncovered, for 1 hour and 15 minutes.

Prepare ahead: Freeze chicken in sauce before baking. Defrost and bake the day of serving.

STYLING AND PHOTOGRAPHY
BY MIRIAM PASCAL COHEN

I couldn't write a *Pesach* cookbook without including the famed Australian dessert that just happens to be... perfect for *Pesach*!

PAVLOVA - DESSERT

Ingredients

4 egg whites

1 cup sugar

1 teaspoon *Pesach* vinegar

2 teaspoons potato starch, sifted

Topping

1 (16-ounce) container nondairy whipped topping

6 strawberries, sliced

2 kiwis, peeled and sliced

Instructions

Preheat the oven to 250°F. Line a baking sheet with parchment paper; set aside. In the bowl of an electric mixer fitted with the whisk attachment, beat egg whites until soft peaks form.

Add sugar, vinegar, and sifted potato starch; beat until a soft, glossy meringue forms.

Pour the meringue onto prepared parchment paper, shaping it into a large circle with a narrow rim. Bake for 1½ hours, or until crisp on the outside. Turn off the oven and allow the meringue to cool inside the oven.

Prepare the topping: In the bowl of an electric mixer fitted with the whisk attachment, beat whipped topping until stiff peaks form.

Spread whipped topping over the cooled meringue shell and fill with fruit.

Cook's Tips: Feel free to replace the strawberries and kiwis with the fruit of your choice.

To make a layered Pavlova as shown in the photo, double both the meringue and whipped topping. No need to double the fruit, as it only goes on the top layer.

Naomi Nachman is a leading kosher food media influencer, cookbook author, and culinary producer. A former Jewish educator, she hosts *Sunny Side Up* on Kosher.com, writes for *Mishpacha* and *The Jewish Home*, and has authored two bestselling ArtScroll cookbooks with over 28,000 copies sold. Naomi appears on major TV networks, leads global culinary programs, serves as CMO of Kosher River Boat Cruises, and shares Jewish food stories worldwide, one bite at a time.

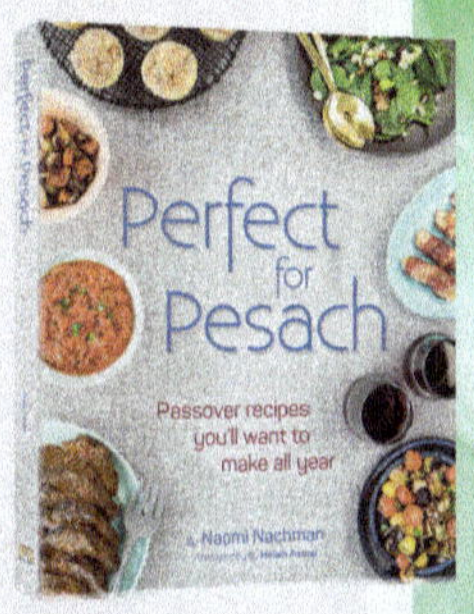

*Recipes reproduced from **Perfect for Pesach** by Naomi Nachman with permission from the copyright holders ArtScroll/Mesorah Publications, LTD.*

Moving Fast in Business is a Superpower —
UNTIL IT ISN'T

BY: AHUVA FISCHER

Entrepreneurs move fast. It's wired into their DNA. They spot opportunities, make decisions, and push forward while others are still weighing the pros and cons. That speed is often exactly what gets a business off the ground and makes it successful in the first place.

But that same trait has a downside: when something is unclear or unstable, moving fast doesn't fix it. It multiplies it.

Without a solid foundation, speed turns small issues into major stressors. A minor delay becomes a crisis. A lack of order becomes constant noise. Eventually, the business starts to feel heavier than it should, pulling you down instead of lifting you up.

When this happens, most business owners assume the answer is to "add" more: more hours, more tools, more hires, more automation. But the real solution is much simpler, and far more effective.

If you've built something real and you want to grow without adding chaos, I use a three-stage framework with my clients:

Stabilize → Optimize → Scale & Grow.

STABILIZE: REMOVE THE BIG STRESSOR

Chaos often doesn't come from the business being "hard." It comes from one significant stressor you've been avoiding. You aren't avoiding it because you're lazy. You're avoiding it because it's annoying, emotional, expensive, or inconvenient.

Once you fix that one thing, you can breathe again. The goal isn't to make sure nothing ever goes wrong. It's to ensure the business (and your life) stop running under constant, draining pressure.

I recently spoke to a successful business owner who opened our call with a sentence I hear more often than you'd think:

"I have so many crises."

She sounded like she was bracing for impact. When we slowed down to review the "crises," we found they weren't dramatic at all: a store sign was arriving a week late, and her secretary was out for the day.

Real issues, yes. Things that needed handling, yes. But these weren't business-ending emergencies.

The real stressor was that there was no clear way to absorb normal disruption, so every minor hiccup escalated directly to her. Because there was no "default way

we handle this," delays turned into panic, absences turned into chaos, and every decision climbed up to the top.

Stabilization is about identifying the one thing weighing the system down and removing it. Sometimes you need an outside perspective, such as a colleague, coach, or advisor, to see what that "one thing" actually is, because you've been living inside it.

OPTIMIZE: BRING ORDER

Once the big stressor is removed, the business gets quieter. Now you have the mental bandwidth for optimization. Optimization isn't about perfection. It's about order.

While every business is unique, here are a few examples of what a healthy, optimized operation looks like:

- Marketing and sales are predictable enough to track and improve
- Projects move forward without you constantly chasing people
- The team is aligned on priorities and knows exactly what "done" looks like
- You understand your cashflow rhythm, planning ahead for both quiet and busy seasons
- Crucially: you and your team can actually take time off without the business descending into chaos

If you have these, you're doing great. But it's normal for many businesses to lack this level of clarity. The reason most business owners fail at this optimization stage is that they try to fix ten messy areas at once.

Instead, pick one area and follow this pattern:

Clarify the process → Delegate ownership → Automate repetition.

A tangible example you can implement today is **centralization**. Stop scattering information across DMs, email threads, and random spreadsheets. Move to a "Single Source of Truth," meaning a centralized workspace like Notion, Monday.com, or ClickUp.

When everyone knows exactly where the "live" data is, they stop re-deciding basic things every day. That eliminates the invisible delays that exhaust your team.

Once you have clarified a process and organized the data, you can look at automation. For example, once your customer support workflow is crystal clear, an AI agent can draft responses to routine inquiries, summarize messages, and escalate only the complex cases to you.

AI and automation cannot create order, but they can reinforce it once it exists.

SCALE & GROW: MULTIPLY WHAT'S WORKING

Only after the business is stabilized and ordered does scaling make sense. Scaling isn't about doing more work. It's about multiplying what already works.

This starts with an analysis of your current results:

What is actually working?
What brings the most value with the least friction?

Once you identify that "gold," you return to your vision:

Where do you want to be in five years? How can you reach more people without burning out?

Scaling is often a matter of shifting your delivery method. Imagine you run powerful workshops that create real transformation for your clients. You don't have to limit yourself to a room of 25 people.

You can multiply that success by offering the workshop online, recording it as a structured digital product, or packaging your proprietary tools into a subscription-based platform. The mission stays the same, but the delivery becomes more scalable.

Similarly, if you run a service-based agency, scaling might mean "productizing" your most successful service. Instead of manual, bespoke labor for every client, you create a standardized Success Roadmap that a trained team can execute.

Growth then feels like wider impact and cleaner systems, not a bigger version of chaos.

BUILD FOR THE LONG HAUL

It is tempting to put a "band-aid" on a problem so you can rush to the next task. But in business, band-aids eventually come off, and the wound reopens, often worse than before.

Real growth comes from slowing down long enough to build a solid foundation. When the business is stabilized and the systems around you are optimized, scaling becomes possible without adding chaos.

You don't need to move slower. You need to build in the right order. Stabilize first, optimize second, and only then scale what's working. This is how the business can carry the growth and give you more freedom, instead of you carrying the business.

Ahuva Fischer helps growing companies where teams are working hard but results have slowed. With over a decade in leadership roles across tech and operations, she identifies operational bottlenecks and helps organizations build clear, scalable ways of working so progress becomes predictable again.

ahuvafisherconsultant.com

THE REAL ART OF NETWORKING

BY: HELENA BAKER

I have spent years hosting networking events and building professional communities, and one thing has become very clear to me. Networking works best when we understand what it is actually for.

At its core, networking is not about selling. It is about relationships. When you approach it from that place, everything becomes simpler, calmer, and far more effective.

When you walk into a networking event, your role is not to pitch, persuade, or convince anyone of anything. Your role is to start conversations that can turn into real relationships over time.

SHOW UP WITH INTENTION

Before you arrive, clarity matters more than confidence. You should know why you are there. Decide how many meaningful conversations you want to have. That number might be five, ten, or fifteen. What matters is that you arrive with intention rather than drifting through the room.

I strongly believe in setting goals for networking events, but not financial goals. Connection goals. Have real conversations. Exchange details. And it is important that you get someone else's details, not just hand out your own. That keeps you in control of the follow up.

Within twenty four hours, you should be arranging a coffee or a short Zoom. The event itself is not where relationships are built. It is simply where they begin.

Over time, those relationships turn into referrals, partnerships, and opportunities. Not because you sold anything, but because trust had the space to develop.

YOU ARE NOT THERE TO SELL

One of the biggest challenges I see, especially with women, is the fear of sounding sales-y. The solution is very simple. Do not sell.

You are not meant to pitch at a networking event. Have a clear one-liner about what you do, say it briefly, and then move on. Ask questions. Shift the focus to the other person.

This requires self discipline. Everyone wants to talk about their business. I certainly do. But networking is not the place to dominate the conversation. If you speak for more than four or five minutes at a time, you are probably losing the other person. I say that as someone who could easily talk for far longer if I did not monitor myself.

I pay close attention to how much space I am taking up. If I notice I have spoken too long, I stop myself and hand the conversation back. That awareness alone can transform the quality of your interactions.

STRUCTURE CREATES SAFETY

I am very intentional about how I run rooms, particularly when many people offer similar services. Personally, I do not believe in competition, but I also understand that not everyone feels that way.

In my regular networking groups, I limit overlap so there is usually one person per industry. In larger events, where that is not possible, structure becomes essential. I use breakout sessions, I intentionally split people up, and I avoid clustering similar professionals together.

If there are many people from the same industry, I say so. That is part of doing business. Confidence comes from trusting your own work and believing that the right people will find you.

NOT EVERY CONVERSATION HAS TO LAND

Here is something that immediately relieves pressure. You are never going to build anything substantial at one networking event. Ever.

Once you accept that, networking becomes far more relaxed.

Your goal in a conversation is not depth. It is direction. You have about fifteen minutes at most. Keep things neutral and respectful. Avoid assumptions about marriage, children, religion, or background. These assumptions are common, and they often shut conversations down without anyone realising it.

Stick to simple questions. Where do you live? What is your biggest business challenge right now? What are you working towards this year?

And if there is no connection, that is completely fine.

There are two things you are looking for in networking. Someone in a complementary or similar space, or someone you naturally click with. If neither is there, you do not need to force it. Not every interaction needs to feel warm or memorable. Some will feel neutral or even slightly awkward. That is a normal part of the process.

NETWORKING WHEN YOU ARE STARTING OUT

If I were starting a business today, I would not begin by networking with strangers. I would start with the people I already know.

Your WhatsApp contacts, your email list, your Facebook connections. That is gold. These people already trust you, and they are far more likely to want to help.

I would invite them for coffee, offer to come to them, offer to pay, and be honest. I am starting this business. These are my challenges. This is what I am thinking. Most people genuinely want to help when they feel trusted and included.

Many early stage founders avoid this because it feels vulnerable. In reality, it is one of the strongest and most effective steps you can take.

STORYTELLING, VISIBILITY, AND BOUNDARIES

I enjoy storytelling. I enjoy writing. And I am very intentional about how I show up.

I am honest in how I communicate. I do not overstate results, manufacture emotion, or say things just to sound impressive.

I do not post for the algorithm at the expense of my self respect. I share honestly, but within clear boundaries. My audience deserves the truth of what it means to run a business, not performance or exaggeration.

That does not mean I avoid difficult topics. I have spoken openly about miscarriage. I have shared honestly about being a war wife with a very young baby at home. But I do not exploit those experiences for attention.

Before anyone starts posting online, I believe they should decide what lines they will not cross. If something feels beyond your comfort level, it is a clear no. Algorithms do not get to change that.

LINKEDIN, INSTAGRAM, AND ALIGNMENT

LinkedIn is still my strongest platform, largely because I have been using it consistently for many years. Results take time.

My advice is simple. Spend time engaging with other people's content. Twenty minutes a day liking and commenting genuinely matters. Do outreach with intention. Not necessarily for sales, but to build relationships that lead to real conversations. Clear weekly goals for meetings make a real difference.

Instagram is more complex for me. There is incredible content there, but much of what performs well is provocative or politically misaligned with how I choose to show up. I do not share my politics online because

it would isolate people, and that is not something I am willing to do.

Instagram has brought positive outcomes. I have sold tickets there. I have had deeply meaningful responses to personal posts. At the same time, I find it challenging, especially from a productivity and mental health perspective.

For me, visibility only works when it is aligned.

At the end of the day, networking is not about being impressive. It is about being intentional, grounded, and allowing relationships to develop naturally over time. Not everything needs to lead somewhere. And that is exactly why the right things do.

Helena Baker is a British-born copywriter who launched her business at 21. After making *aliyah* four years ago, she pioneered English-speaking networking in Israel. Today she runs three thriving groups with 75 members and an annual mega event, and produces high-level community events for Monday.com, PwC, and Rothschild & to name just a few to create high-level, niche community networking events.

🌐 englishspeakingnetworking.com
🌐 helenabaker.com